Progress in Planning, Vol. 39, pp. 167–242, 1993.
Printed in Great Britain. All rights reserved.

Contents

Abstract

How does participation work in a situation of cultural pluralism in terms of meeting pluralist needs? This is the major question on which the monograph focuses. This issue is analysed by investigating relationships between ethnic groups in a situation of pluralism. Specifically this monograph examines the relationships between the Negev Bedouin and the Israeli authorities. The Bedouin are a previously nomadic ethnic minority who have become sedentarised in spontaneous or planned settlements. Their participation in their relocation in Tel Malhata is the focus of the case study.

Within the debate around cultural and political pluralism, this research examines the concept of pluralist needs, embracing both ethnic and citizen needs, together with their definition in a context of discrimination, and creates methodological tools which are used to evaluate government policies and plans towards the ethnic minorities. The case study example of majority–minority relationships is analysed through the settlement planning process, focusing on the complexities of planning in a situation of conflicting needs. The role of participation in addressing ethnic and citizen needs is also examined to illustrate the complexities of meeting pluralist needs.

The major conclusion points to the value of realising pluralist needs in planning and development schemes for ethnic minority groups. Such an approach would greatly ease the process of social change, while fostering the stability of the society as a whole.

Acknowledgements

This monograph is part of a PH.D. dissertation undertaken at the London School of Economics and Political Science. I would like to thank my supervisors, Dr C. Moser and Professor D. Diamond for their strong support and encouragement during the process of undertaking this research.

Preface

The relationship between majority–minority groups in planning and development schemes is the focus of this monograph, with particular attention paid to pluralism, needs and participation in development.

Most of the analysis presented in this monograph is based on the extensive research carried out on Bedouin settlements in the Negev region of Israel. The basic premise in this monograph is that debates around majority–minority relationships have generic characteristics which could be extended to every country where ethnic minorities exist. This includes almost every country in the world.

The debates are not necessarily objective. They can be analysed from different viewpoints, each of which expresses the different values of the researcher. I have chosen to analyse majority–minority relationships from a perspective where optimum pluralism would be achieved in development schemes by interweaving majority and minority needs. This follows my belief that such an approach is the only way to heal the constant conflicts which occur in many of these countries.

How do we translate cultural pluralism and ethnicity into planning schemes so that a stable and viable environment can be created? What are the best ways to plan so that both majority and minority needs are met to the satisfaction of both sides? These very complicated and sensitive issues are the core of this monograph.

CHAPTER 1

Introduction

1.1. AIMS AND SCOPE

While there exists a growing awareness of the important role that different cultural, social and political characteristics of Third World societies play in development projects, academics' and policy-makers' awareness of the issue of 'pluralism, ethnicity and development' has not yet been translated into planning practice. The lack of adequate and clear cut operational frameworks addressing minority groups' needs in many areas of the world, characterises the vagueness and controversy that already exists regarding this issue.

The aim of the monograph is to contribute to a new perspective which, by allowing for greater pluralism by policy-makers and planners will, it is hoped, dispel some of the vagueness surrounding these problems as they exist in many countries including Israel. These issues are discussed through the analysis of the relationship between the Negev Bedouin and Israeli authorities as well as other examples of development projects in which ethnic groups are involved. The whole debate around pluralism and ethnicity in development is placed within the context of the settlement planning process, where majority–minority needs are spatially expressed. The role of participation, both as an institutional and management issue, in the settlement planning process is another dynamic examined in this monograph, highlighting the influence of the heterogeneity of the beneficiaries as well as politicians and planners on the nature of participation and its outcomes. This is a new dimension of the issue of participation about which not enough has been written.

1.2. THE STRUCTURE OF THE MONOGRAPH

The monograph which follows has three parts. In the first part, by way of a background, the majority–minority relationships in Israeli society are presented together with a short background on the Bedouin situation in Israel. Part 2 highlights the existing debates around cultural and political pluralism, needs and

175

basic needs strategy and the concept of participation in development. All prove to be interrelated when attempting to formulate a conceptual framework for pluralism and development.

In Part 3 the whole debate around pluralism and ethnicity in planning and development is analysed. It throws a new light on ethnicity and development, the citizen and ethnic needs and their use in planning and evaluation of plans. The new concepts of pluralist needs, including both ethnic and citizen needs and their definition in the context of discrimination against a minority are presented in Part 3. For the purpose of planning, these are then translated into methodological tools which are employed to evaluate government or other agencies policies and plans. The practical dimensions of these rather new planning tools are used to analyse the settlement planning process of the Bedouin in the Negev and other case studies. Part 4 concludes by highlighting some of the fundamental steps needed to carry out a planning process which would integrate both majority and minority's needs in development.

1.3. ISRAELI SOCIETY

Israeli society encompasses a strong mixture of social, economic, ethnic and religious divisions. Smooha (1978) distinguishes in particular five of the major divisions: Askenazi/Oriental Jews, religious/non-religious Jews, Israeli Arabs/Jews, Druze/Christian/Moslem Israeli Arabs, and Palestinians/Jews. Any discussion about pluralism, ethnicity and planning which aims to meet the needs of the various ethnic groups in any country can only be presented if it considers the complexities of ethnic relationships within one political unit. The example in this section focuses on the complexities of ethnic relationships between the various groups within Israeli society in its formulation and the way conflicting needs influenced planning and development.

This section takes a brief look at the historical background which led to the creation of the Jewish state in 1948 and goes on to demonstrate the lack of preparedness and foresight on the part of Israeli policy-makers to deal with all the cultural complexities in the face of the galvanising ideals of Zionism.

The idea of Zionism is rooted in the mid-19th century. It came about in reaction to anti-semitism and the persecution which Jews still faced in Western and Eastern Europe in spite of the new liberal democratic movements and the waves of emancipation which followed. Paradoxically, even the boldest spokesmen of the socialist movements in Europe argued against providing national status and civil rights to Jews. The Jews were expected to assimilate and were uniquely overlooked as a people deserving self-determination (Tsur, 1976). With anti-semitism on the one hand and the tide of emancipation on the other, Jewish leaders came to the conclusion that the Jewish problem required a political solution which would provide a place in which Jews could live as Jews according to their religion, and be treated as equal citizens.

Theodore Herzl was one of the first to promote the political solution of the creation of a Jewish state. These ideas are expressed in his book 'Altneuland' (The Old–New Land), in which he emphasises the fact that the Jewish problem was not only religious or social, but national and political. In his book he outlined the principles of the new state, gave details pertaining to the economic basis of the state, and a land policy in which he recommended that lands be publicly controlled. In fact, the way in which these principles were implemented later became the core of the socio-economic and political conflicts between the various divisions in Israeli society, and the strength of political ideals and religious tradition masked many of the problems which were to arise.

After considering other locations for the Jewish state, Hertzl reached the conclusion that the only place in which a Jewish state could be established was in Palestine. Why? Zionism had to take into account the historical fact that the Jews were exiled from Israel, and biblical prophecy foresaw the day when the Jews would return to their land.

> "The distinguishing characteristic of the Jews has been their Exile. From one, obvious angle of vision they could see their exile as the part forcible, part revolutionary removal of the Jews from Eretz Israel — the land of Israel — and the loss of all political rights over their country in the wake of the failure of the last bloody revolt against Rome. And thus conceived, the restoration of the Jews to Eretz Israel implied, above all else, Redemption."
>
> (Vital, 1975, p. 3)

But the idea of the return of the Jewish people would bring about a great conflict with the Arabs who already lived in the country. Few Jewish leaders and individual thinkers directed attention towards the Arabs living in Palestine during the development of Zionism. But what all their ideas had in common was the desire of Zionism to create a separate social, economic, political and cultural Jewish community. The Zionist leaders all believed that this was a precondition in creating a strong nation. This is an example of how contradictory needs were formed, and how, from the beginning, principles of pluralism could not be adopted because they were considered a threat to a strong Jewish nation.

However, the attitude towards the Arabs among Zionist leaders was not unified. Gorni (1979) distinguishes between four main attitudes: the integrationist altruistic approach which called for cooperation with the Arabs and emphasised the fact that the country belongs to both nations, Jewish and Arab; the opposite approach, the separatist approach which rejected cooperation with Arabs and believed in inevitable conflict between the two nations; the liberal pragmatic approach which called for a cautious and fair attitude towards the Arabs — collaboration involving the Arabs only through their leaders and full equal rights for the two nations; and the social conservative approach which tried to create a synthesis between Zionism and socialism. This last approach was dominant in the Zionist movement.

But it revealed contradictions between the two ideologies. The class principles of socialism clashed with the nationalist principles of Zionism.

Of course whatever the approach, there still remained the conflict between the historical right of the Jewish people to return to the land of Israel, which the Zionists believed in, and the historical reality of previous Arab settlement of the country. Ben Gurion, one of the Zionist leaders and later the first Prime Minister of Israel, defined the essence of the conflict perfectly: "Eretz Israel — the place of birth of the Jewish nation — the place of residence for the Arabs".

The implementation of Zionist principles as the basis for the establishment of a Jewish state contradicted with the interests of other groups within Israeli society.

Golaney (1979) identifies several planning principles which grew out of Zionist ideology, which he terms Israeli ideology. They were: first, the need to create a new and strong nation out of people who had a common history but had been dispersed around the world; second, the need for diversified employment, based on agriculture, for the creation of a healthy economy and for the evolution of new social values (also in Akzin and Dror, 1966); third, the preservation of land suitable for agriculture; fourth, a society rooted in the land of the Bible which emphasises continuity between the past, present and future culture; fifth, an equal distribution of the Jewish population all over the country. The sixth point deals with the establishment of new, mainly rural settlements in less densely populated regions. The last relates to gearing education towards national, physical, spiritual and economic survival.

But what the implementation of the principles of Zionism after the creation of the state of Israel neglected to focus on was the needs of the different groups in Israeli society. The preservation of lands, the dispersion of the Jewish population and the creation of new rural settlements led to a conflict over landownership with Arabs and Bedouins in Israel, because their own needs were not recognised.

Another challenge, the absorption of Jewish immigrants which was one of the major principles of Zionism, was conducted with a western, Askenazi approach, and, rather than encouraging participation on the part of Oriental Jews, their cultural needs were largely ignored. The massive influx of immigrants which arrived in the country after its creation in 1948 consisted of people from some 100 different countries. These were the survivors of the holocaust from Europe, Jews from Western Europe, and Oriental Jews from Asian and African countries. From 1953 to 1966 the state grew 2.5 fold.

The manner of absorption of immigrants in Israel during the 1950s amply illustrates the argument that the ignorance of different needs of different cultural groups leads to failure of policies and plans. The implementation of the Zionist principle of 'ingathering the exiles' was made in such a way that the different needs of Oriental Jews were denied almost completely, and absorption policies were regarded by many as a dismal failure. This fact was later to lead to great social conflict between Oriental and Western Jews, and with the heavy-handed policies of the Zionist leaders toward their own people, it is little wonder that much insensitivity was also displayed toward Arab and Bedouin.

Being Moslems by religion, the Bedouin in Israel formed another non-Jewish division within Israeli society. But the Israeli authorities approached the Bedouin society differently from the Arabs. Unlike the Arabs who were considered totally hostile, the Bedouin were considered as loyal to the state's principles. Some Bedouin also served in the army force. Their identification with the State of Israel eased to a certain extent the suspicion characterising the Jewish attitude towards the Arabs. Yet, on landownership matters, they faced the same type of discrimination and sense of conflict with the authorities as the Arabs, as seen later in Part 3.

1.4. THE BEDOUIN SOCIETY IN ISRAEL — BACKGROUND INFORMATION

Bedouin society is one of the non-Jewish segments within Israeli society. Their roots are in a nomadic lifestyle which they maintained up to the beginning of the 19th century. They are Muslim by religion and speak Arabic, but they are a clearly separate community from Israeli Arabs, as they have gone through different stages of transition from nomadic and semi-nomadic life to sedentarisation. As mentioned earlier they also have a different relationship with the Israeli authorities, being considered a more loyal group and serving in the Israeli Defence Forces. Yet, on many issues they suffer the same discrimination and go through the same type of conflict with the authorities as other minority groups.

Towards the end of the British Mandate in 1948; the Bedouin were divided into 95 tribes. The statistical divisions were made according to the official definition of a tribe made by the British authorities, recognising territorial and administrative units led by chiefs whom the authorities viewed as official representatives of their followers. After 1948, with the creation of the State of Israel, only 11,000 Bedouin remained in the Negev, the rest escaping to Jordan. Their number has increased since, with the death rate going down and the birth rate remaining high.

The social structure of nomadic societies has specific functions in a nomadic lifestyle. Their clear cut social grouping usually reflects kinship relationships. Nomadic social structure functions in a hierarchy: kinship groups gather into tribes and tribes gather into groups of tribes which together form confederations. Once nomadic societies sedentarise, the relationships between social groups and within groups are changed, and this is no less the case with the Bedouin. The changes in social structure which they have been undergoing from the beginning of this century are most evident in the declining importance of the tribes within the hierarchical structure, and the changing role of the sheikhs.

The process of sedentarisation has also altered the relationships between the three major social groups of Bedouin society: the 'real' Bedouin, the Fellahin (peasants) and the Abid (slaves). The 'real' Bedouin are descended from nomadic ancestors from Saudi Arabia and have moved through the Sinai Peninsula to the Negev. They always considered themselves superior to the Fellahin and the masters of the desert. The 'Fellahin' (peasants) joined the 'real' Bedouin in the mid-19th century as agricultural workers. They were subordinate to the 'real' Bedouin and were landless. Eventually some of them purchased land from the 'real' Bedouin. This made them more economically independent but did not change their status. The third group is the Abid group, the black slaves which are considered inferior to the two mentioned groups. The development dynamics between these groups will be examined carefully in Part 3.

Administratively, the Negev is included within the district of the city of Be'er Sheva. This administrative division was established in Ottoman times at the beginning of the 20th century and was designed to coincide more or less with the areas occupied predominantly by nomadic Bedouin. An administrative centre at Be'er Sheva was established in the year 1900 to facilitate Ottoman rule over the nomads.

The Bedouin ceased wandering during the British Mandate in Palestine. From this period they settled in spontaneous settlements, and by the mid 1960s some of them had moved to planned settlements which the Israeli government built for them. In 1988, 35% of them were living in planned settlements, with the rest living in spontaneous settlements scattered over an area of approximately 1.5 million dunam (150,000 hectares) in the Northern Negev.

The case study presented in this monograph is based on a settlement planning procedure in which Bedouin were involved, which occurred between 1980–1983 in which some 500 Bedouin families were evacuated and re-settled by a special arrangement with the Israeli Government. This arrangement was based on a landownership law which determined the financial compensations to be paid for their lands and the planning and implementation of replaced settlements for the evacuated Bedouin in Kessifa and Aruar. Initially, the Bedouin strongly objected to the evacuation of their lands mainly because the compensation offered to them was not sufficient. The government then formed new bodies, the Bedouin Team and the Implementation Authority (see details in Section 3.5). The two bodies, each on their own, negotiated with the Bedouin on the revision of the Landownership Law and the settlement planning process. Much of the methodology developed in this monograph is based on the analysis of this project, which clearly illustrates the concepts of ethnicity and planning within the context of pluralism.

CHAPTER 2

Conceptual Framework: Pluralism, Needs, Participation

2.1. THE CONCEPT OF CULTURAL PLURALISM

Pluralism is a common feature to many First, Second and Third World countries. It is often used simply as a synonym for social or political diversity (Dahl, 1980). Pluralism as a concept is one of the more complicated issues to deal with, as it has several separate meanings in different fields of studies, which have changed with time (Clarke *et al.*, 1984). Smooha specifies the social or cultural meaning of pluralism:

> "Pluralism is a central structural feature of total societies. It is a continuous, multi-dimensional phenomenon, manifesting in two main aspects, i.e. cultural diversity and social separation. Although these two dimensions tend to overlap, they should be distinguished because the degree of their divergence is quite significant."
>
> (Smooha, 1978, p. 14)

These two aspects of pluralism — cultural diversity and social separation — express the complex position of ethnic groups in a situation of pluralism. This complex position is reflected in formulating planning procedures for such groups and is one of the major problems of planning processes.

'Political pluralism' is the most fashionable of the latest approaches. This school's development is associated with Shils (1956), Dahl (1980) and Kornhauser (1960). They consider pluralism as a basis for democracy in Western societies.

> "The struggle of individuals and groups to gain autonomy in relation to the control of others is, like the efforts to acquire control over others, a fundamental tendency of political life. Struggles for autonomy result from conflicts and cleavages, and when these struggles are successful, as they are, they result in turn in tendencies towards pluralism. Because conflicts and cleavages are ubiquitous, so too are tendencies of pluralism."
>
> (Dahl, 1980, p. 20)

Dahl mentions that although pluralism is a "necessary condition" — an essential characteristic and a consequence of a democratic regime — pluralism also creates problems which result from discrimination on the base of democratic principles for which no satisfactory solutions seem to have been found. The case of the Bedouin in Israel or minority ethnic groups such as the blacks in Great Britain or the Puerto Ricans in the U.S.A. provide such examples.

Pluralism in political sciences is also called 'organisational pluralism'. This actually refers to the diversity and autonomy of organisations which exist in

181

democratic regimes. This diversity must be taken into account in order to analyse conflict among a given collection of people. The greater the number of organisations and the greater their autonomy, the greater the organisational pluralism.

Another use of pluralism in the social sciences is the use of the term 'cultural pluralism'. This refers to the studies of ethnic or racial issues, especially as applied in the United States. This approach has been mainly developed by Glazer (1982), Moynihan (1975) and Gordon (1964).

Historically speaking, Furnivall was the first to introduce the concept of a 'plural society'. This concept is associated with developing regions. As an economist and a colonial administrator in South-East Asia, he defined a plural society as:

> "comprising two or more elements or social orders which live side by side, yet without mingling, in one political unit."
>
> (Furnivall, 1939, p. 446)

For Furnivall, pluralism implied a dominancy of alien minority over an indigenous majority. The two elements create social diversity. The reason for this social diversity is ascribed, according to Furnivall, to a lack of "common social demands." This means that the various communities within the plural society possess cultural values which are incompatible with the cultural values of other communities.

The major contribution of Furnivall, according to Rabushka (1972), is in his observation that plural societies are qualitatively distinct from homogeneous societies, and the only common ground in the different communities of a plural society is in the market place. In his observation, that external force is required to maintain order, Furnivall assumes that plural societies contain violent conflict within their social structure.

Smith sharpens the conflict element in Furnivall's definition of plural society. He expands Furnivall's economic colonial concept of plural society to include all societies, colonial or other, that share two conditions: incompatible institutions and rule by a cultural minority (Smooha, 1978). His concept of plural society refers to domination of a cultural minority by the rest of society:

> "Given the fundamental differences of belief, value and organizations that connote pluralism, the monopoly of power by one cultural section is the essential precondition for the maintenance of the total society in its current form."
>
> (Smith, 1965, p. 86)

Cultural pluralism is a major determinant in the structure of the plural society. Smith (1965) defines cultural pluralism as the coexistence of different cultural traditions in a population, each possessing different forms of institution, such as marriage, family, education, religion and economy. Culturally, differentiated communities usually vary in their institutional devices, systems of beliefs, values and social organisation. A plural society with sharp cultural pluralism is thus a unit only in the political sense. According to Smith it is cultural pluralism that imposes the necessity for domination by one cultural section over the others. It is for the maintenance of political order in this inclusive unit that domination is needed, and regulations to maintain, control and coordinate the plural society are used.

Smith, nevertheless, emphasises that not all diverse cultures are plural societies. There are differences in the degree of cultural pluralism which influence the degree of incompatibility between institutions existing within them (Smith, 1965). By contrast, there are also pluralistic societies in which value systems are compatible in spite of cultural diversity. These are systems that permit a significant measure of autonomy to important units or sub-units (Dahl, 1980). Brazil and the United States are two examples of such pluralistic societies according to Smith. Kuper in his definition of pluralism relates the term to:

> "societies characterized by certain conditions of cultural diversity and social cleavage, in whatever way these conditions of social and cultural pluralism arise, from the contact of different peoples and cultures within a single society."
>
> (Kuper, 1969, p. 3)

Kuper also differentiates between two distinctive traditions of pluralism. The first tradition relates to Smith's theory of plural society. The stability of the society, according to this theory, is threatened by sharp cleavages between the different social sections. The relationships between the social sections are characterised by inequalities. Kuper calls this the "conflict model" of plural societies. The second tradition is much older. It offers the concept of a pluralistic society in which the differences between the social groups are integrated in a balanced adjustment which provides conditions for 'stable democratic government'. This is the 'equilibrium' model of pluralism. In addition, Kuper suggests a synthesis of the two, which he calls "problems of social change", which suggests another view of societies undergoing evolution from cultural pluralism and divisive conflict to political pluralism and equilibrium (Kuper, 1969).

Proponents of the 'equilibrium' model of political pluralism are associated with concepts of democracy and liberalism. Shils (1956) and Kornhouser (1960) lead the discussion of pluralistic societies to consider liberal democracy. Kornhouser argues that a pluralistic society supports liberal democracy. Hence, the political structure in pluralistic societies is plural itself. There is a clear separation of power between the executive, the legislative, the administrative and the judiciary branches. This is the basis for democratic rule. Besides this clear separation between the political sectors, Kornhouser (1960) points out the necessity for strong and stable independent groups which function as mediators between the individual and the state.

Integration, a key factor in the pluralistic society, is effected by 'multiple affiliations'. 'Multiple affiliation' is a further pre-condition for pluralism, according to Kornhauser (1960), where multiple associations must embrace ethnicity. This definition expands the concept of pluralism to individual pluralism in the sense of individual participation, fostering diversity of interests, discouraging exclusive loyalties and linking the plural structure together by personal ties and relationships. It may also be expected to contribute to integration by emphasising common values (Kuper, 1969).

Integration occurs only when there exists a commitment to common values such as: sentiments of communal affinity, respect for the law, moderation in political involvement, and the recognition of the dignity of other values and activities within the society (Shils, 1956). However, integration in a pluralistic society does not necessarily lead to consensus, precisely because of the diversity of values between the various groups.

The 'conflict' model of plural societies approaches a society from a different angle. As mentioned earlier, it is based on Furnivall's argument that the political form of the plural society is one of colonial domination, which imposes a western superstructure of administration and business on the native environment, and a forced unity on the different segments of the population (Furnivall, 1939).

Unlike the pluralistic model of society which emphasises communality and integration between the different sections of the population, the plural model emphasises the separate characteristics of the social groups and the fact that each group holds on to its own religion, culture, language and ideas. Cultural diversity and social divisions characterise the social foundation of the plural society (Kuper, 1969).

The plural society supposes a repression of subordinate sections of that society, in contrast to the democratic nature of a pluralistic form of society, which expresses itself in the political representation of ethnic groups in political institutions. The repression of these groups is a condition of political unity. Repression must exist in order to avoid the growth of separate societies as a result of the different ethnic groups within the plural society pursuing their different institutions and practices.

Integration according to the 'conflict model' of plural society is imposed by the colonial power and the force of economic circumstances. In a plural society, racial differences are likely to be transformed into racial tensions. Hence, plural societies are held together by regulations, and not by integration.

Smith's major contribution is associated with his distinction between two mechanisms: that of integration which occurs in a pluralistic society, and that of regulation which functions in a plural society (Kuper, 1969).

Other distinctions between two basic types of society are suggested by Kuper:

> "Integrated societies are characterized by consensus and cultural homogeneity, and regulated societies are characterized by dissensus and cultural pluralism."
>
> (Kuper, 1969, p. 14)

This implies that cultural homogeneity (or heterogeneity) is inevitable in democratic forms of government and suggests that many of the newly independent states may either dissolve into separate cultural divisions or maintain their identity but only under conditions of domination and subordination between groups. The case of the Bedouin in Israel is connected to the second situation.

2.1.1. Cultural pluralism and ethnicity

'Cultural pluralism' is associated with studies of the ethnic or racial issues, especially as they are applied in the United States. This approach is developed by Gordon (1964) and Glazer and Moynihan (1975). Glazer connects cultural pluralism with the concept of assimilation and acculturation in the United States. In his article, "The Problem of Ethnic Studies", published in 1982, he concentrates his analysis on the implications of cultural pluralism and ethnicity for education. But first he discusses the association of cultural pluralism with assimilation, acculturation or Americanisation. These concepts were very popular in the United States up to the 1940s. But today these policies seem interpreted as a form of "domestic colonialism and imperialism" (Glazer, 1982). Critiques on these policies argue that the Americans had no intention of really integrating immigrants as equals, even when these people were stripped of their original cultures. In fact they were not allowed entry into American society on equal terms. However, the process of assimilation and acculturation is still seen as a positive process by many liberal analysts.

> "Assimilation was a desirable consequence of the reduction of prejudice and discrimination, while acculturation, that is, becoming more like the majority, would contribute to the reduction of discrimination and prejudice."
>
> (Glazer, 1982, p. 100)

The question which is raised by Glazer relates to the blindness of the proponents of assimilation — to the fact that groups or elements would want to preserve their cultural identities, even if prejudice and discrimination disappeared. This blindness may be the result of positive motives: the immediate concern for the economic and social position of these groups.

> "How could they make the transition to a better position? First by becoming more like other Americans, and then by persuading other Americans to abandon prejudice and discrimination on the grounds that the ethnic groups and different races were really just like them anyway."
>
> (Glazer, 1982, p. 101)

There was a great deal of propaganda in the U.S.A. during the 1930s against discrimination and hostility, but this created misunderstandings:

> "This strategy seemed to be reasonable, but as time went on it created confusion between the point of view within liberalism that argues: 'They are just like everyone else, so they should not be objects of prejudice and discrimination', and the one that asserts, 'they are different and have a right to be different, and this difference does not justify any antagonism.'"
>
> (Glazer, 1982, p. 102)

The two World Wars halted the development of cultural pluralism in this direction. During this period 'ethnic loyalties' were considered as negative expressions. It was only after the Second World War that cultural pluralism penetrated into the education system. The issue of 'intercultural education' was raised. The basic premise in the 'intercultural education' approach also finally recognised the dual identity of ethnic groups:

> "There were two themes in intercultural education: the first was that one should not be ashamed of one's heritage; the second and more important was that all should be tolerant of racial, religious and cultural differences."
>
> (Glazer, 1982, p. 104)

The 'multi-ethnic education', a curriculum guideline, which was published in 1976, went further, emphasising the dual position of ethnic groups. This is manifested in the following four principles:

> "1. Ethnic diversity should be recognized and respected at individual, group, and societal levels.
> 2. Ethnic diversity provides a basis for societal cohesiveness and survival.
> 3. Equality of opportunity should be afforded to members of all ethnic groups.
> 4. Ethnic identification should be optional for individuals."
>
> (Glazer, 1982, p. 107)

These principles were determined by ethnic minorities' demands for recognition. Unlike the old 'intercultural education' approach, the new 'multi-ethnic' approach emphasised recognition rather than mere tolerance. It emphasised recognition of the ethnic identity of ethnic groups. At the same time there was also emphasis on equality of opportunity — in this case in education, but it could be applied to equal occupational opportunities as well (Glazer, 1982).

The basic principle of the new cultural pluralism was therefore:

> "not based on the desire for a transitional period of tolerance to ease the way to full acculturation and assimilation. Instead it is based on the assumption or expectation that separate groups in the United States will continue to exist, that they have value, and that there are both pragmatic and moral reasons why the government should provide some assistance to their maintenance."
>
> (Glazer, 1982, p. 111)

Some black and other minority groups in the United States demanded, at a certain point, separate territories under the control of each group. The demand for separatism, as Glazer explains, resulted from the way ethnic minorities were defined. The definition of blacks, Mexican Americans, and Puerto Ricans as colonial people has a totally different connotation than a definition of them as the object of discrimination or prejudice. In the former case the connotation of colonial groups means that they should be freed, whereas in the latter case it suggests that discrimination should be banned. Glazer differentiates between "weak" cultural pluralism and "strong" cultural pluralism as two extremes. 'Weak' cultural pluralism is a kind of tolerance which leads to acculturation and assimilation. 'Strong' cultural pluralism is primarily based on ideological viewpoints of the position of racial and ethnic groups in American life. It emphasises the colonial status and the repression of the ethnic group's culture by Anglo-Americans (Glazer, 1982).

Therefore, 'strong' cultural pluralism contained a threat to states because of its association with separatism, where extremely diversified groups could demand geo-political separation, and pluralism would break down. Glazer suggests an intermediate term, "integration", which stands between the two extremes. By this definition of integration he expresses his view regarding cultural pluralism in the educational system in society:

> "we should not support the creation of sharp differences, with children of an ethnic background, neatly labelled and numbered, automatically taking special courses in that background. The society should be open to those who have no interest in a background defined by their descent, and have no desire to maintain it or make claims for it; but it should also be open to those who do take interest in their background and wish to maintain it and instill it in their children."
>
> (Glazer, 1982, p. 123)

While Glazer emphasises cultural pluralism that seeks to be tolerant of the dual identity of ethnic groups in educational systems, this monograph aims to focus on the implications of cultural pluralism on approaches to the development of settlement planning (with the example of ethnic groups in Israel). Here, the approach adopted was that of assimilating ethnic groups while ignoring their cultural identity, especially for the Oriental Jews and also in the case of Bedouin society. It was expressed in inappropriate policies and plans proposed for these ethnic groups, and this aspect of the issue is analysed in the following chapters.

In order to translate the concept of pluralism and ethnicity into an operational framework of planning, it will be connected with the debate around needs in development projects and the participation of beneficiaries in the planning process. A brief discussion around needs and participation is presented in the next two sections.

2.2. BASIC NEEDS AND DEVELOPMENT

The use in planning of the concept of the 'needs' of Third World societies gained widespread currency in the early 1970s when international agencies such as the ILO and the World Bank became aware of the necessity to introduce policies which aimed to reduce subsistence poverty and inequality (Chanery *et al.*, 1974). These ideas were then integrated into the basic needs approach, a new strategy to combine the supposedly antithetical ideals of growth and equity. The basic needs approach calls for tackling, in many development projects, the issues of malnutrition, debilitating disease, inadequate housing and lack of access to essential services such as drinking water, sanitation, health care and education (Streeton, 1981).

What constitutes 'basic needs' is understood in various ways, according to who identifies those needs. The minimum interpretation alludes only to narrow physical needs like food, clothing, shelter, water and basic education. Another interpretation relates also to satisfying beneficiaries' wants, as they themselves, rather than external specialists, perceive them. This means that people should automatically have the opportunity to earn wages providing them an income to purchase the goods and services they want. Finally, the broadest interpretation emphasises not only economic and material elements of autonomy, but also embraces individual and group participation in the formulation and implementation of projects (Streeten, 1981, p. 26). This wider interpretation is the most radical and revolutionary, calling as it does for the redistribution not only of income and assets but also of power, which is seen by this group as the essence of basic needs and as fundamental to human rights.

While this concept of basic needs provides a comprehensive framework for development, there remains the question of how these needs are perceived by the policy-makers who provide the solutions, especially when these solutions involve satisfying minority ethnic groups' needs. It is quite obvious that in such cases, policy-makers, who usually belong to different cultural, social or ethnic groupings, would have a different perception of these needs from those of the ethnic groups' members themselves. In this case the participation of ethnic groups in the planning process becomes essential to ensure successful results.

2.3. PARTICIPATION IN MEETING ETHNIC GROUP NEEDS

The participation of ethnic groups in different stages of development projects is a crucial component in the settlement planning process under principles of pluralism.

Although its importance is now widely recognised both conceptually and in its role in development projects, there is no clear consensus as to what is meant by community participation. Different definitions exist, each reflecting ideological interpretations of development and different approaches to planning (Moser, 1989b; Midgley, 1986). The participation of the Bedouin in the Israeli Negev in the project involving their re-settlement provides a useful example of the complexity of defining participation, distinguishing between its various objectives and determining its procedures so that successful results are obtained.

The idea of participation is based on western democratic theory, according to which ordinary citizens have a right to share in decision-making. This inspiration is reflected in a variant of liberal democratic theory, known as neighbourhood democracy, which advocates the creation of small scale institutions in villages and urban neighbourhoods of the Third World (Midgley, 1986).

Popular participation is therefore viewed in the context of the basic democratic principle that people should have the right to be involved in their own development (Conyers, 1982). This is mainly advocated by nations of the Third World which have recently been granted independence. Theoretically, participation could become one of the key-notes of political pluralism, especially as reflected in the pluralistic model of society. Kuper in his model of 'equilibrium' discusses the changes in the social forms of such societies. The change is expressed in a shift from domination by a racial or cultural minority to democratic government based on participation of groups (Kuper, 1969).

Participation is a complex issue which raises frequent debate resulting from different and sometimes contradictory idealogical interpretations and approaches to planning. As participation is a multi-dimensional concept, and as the act of participation is never neutral, it is impossible to present it in any single form (Oakley and Marsden, 1984). It is therefore suggested that the discussion on participation be focused on four main questions: 'Why participation?', 'When participation?', 'Whose participation?' and 'How participation?' (Moser, 1989b). These questions are useful in clarifying the complexity of the participation process especially of ethnic groups under principles of pluralism.

2.3.1. Why participation? — definitions of community participation

No clear cut consensus exists among development scholars and practitioners as to what is meant by community participation. Definitions of community participation vary largely by using a wide range of terms which basically reflect ideological approaches to development and planning, and explanations of social processes (Oakley and Marsden, 1984; Moser, 1983, 1989b). The lack of consensus results in different objectives where community participation is used as an approach.

While there is no point in simply reproducing a list of the large number of definitions which exist in literature, it seems useful to analyse the different interpretations of community participation to discover their main characteristics.

The United Nations Economic and Social Council Resolution No. 1929 states that:

> "Participation requires the voluntary and democratic involvement of people in:
> a. Contributing to the development effort. b. Sharing equitably in benefits derived
> therefrom. c. Decision-making in respect of setting goals, formulating policies and
> planning and implementing economic and social development programs."
>
> (Midgley, 1986, p. 25)

These components seem to be too general, naive and sometimes unrealistic to implement, and yet they are, partly or all, basic principles in a large number of definitions which vary according to approaches of development. While development economists tend to define community participation in terms of the equitable sharing of the benefits of projects, social planners may define it in terms of contribution to the development effort, or the role of community participation in the decision-making process in projects which affect their life.

This latter definition clearly reveals the role of participation in squatter settlements upgrading projects. There, community participation is defined as:

> "the voluntary and democratic involvement of beneficiaries in contributing to the execution of the project, in sharing the benefits derived therefrom and in making decisions with respect to setting goals, formulating the project and implementing the plans."
>
> (Habitat, 1985, p. 3)

Oakley and Marsden (1984) list in a continuum the more common interpretations of community participation. On the one hand participation is a voluntary contribution to projects without people's influence on the shape of the project. On the other, participation is an active process to increase control.

Paul defines community participation as:

> "an active process by which beneficiaries influence the direction and execution of a development project with a view to enhancing their well-being in terms of income, personal growth, self-reliance or other values they cherish."
>
> (Paul, 1986, p. 2)

Paul's definition may refer to community participation which is not spontaneous or 'bottom up', but induced, coerced, or 'top down'. This distinction has been made by the United Nations. While coerced participation is condemned and induced participation is regarded as second best, spontaneous participation or 'bottom up' participation:

> "comes closest to the ideal mode of participation as it reflects voluntary and autonomous action on the part of the people to organize and deal with their problems unaided by governments or other external agencies."
>
> (United Nations, 1981, p. 8)

Midgley (1986) makes a similar distinction between 'authentic' participation, in which all three elements mentioned earlier in the UN quote exist, and 'pseudo' participation, in which implementation is based on decisions already taken by others. These distinctions obviously relate to the question of the rationale behind the inclusion of participation in development projects.

2.3.2. Why participation? — objectives of community participation

> "Participation in the development process would improve understanding of what people wanted, help in ordering of their priorities, and raise their commitment to any improvements that were made."
>
> (Gilbert and Ward, 1984, p. 771)

This objective of participation includes some of the many interpretations of the reasons for and causes of participation which illustrate both the confusion around this issue and also the growing awareness of its importance, especially in international organisations such as the ILO and UNICEF (Moser, 1989b).

One of the ways to distinguish the objectives of participation in projects is by making a twofold distinction between definitions of participation (Moser, 1989b): participation which includes an element of empowerment, and participation which does not. Yet, it is not clear what is meant by empowerment, and one of the methods to 'measure' empowerment in participatory projects has been through making a distinction between participation as a means and participation as an end.

> "Where participation is interpreted as a means, it generally becomes a form of mobilization to get things done. This equally can be state-directed, top down mobilization (sometimes enforced) to achieve specific objectives, or bottom up 'voluntary' community-based mobilization to obtain a larger immediate share of resources. Where participation is identified as an end, the objective is not a fixed quantifiable development goal but a process whose outcome is an increasingly 'meaningful' participation in the development process."
>
> (Moser, 1983, p. 3)

However, the distinction as to whether participation is used as a means or an end is mechanistic and limited. It is more meaningful to point out the process whereby participation as a means has the capacity to develop into participation as an end. For this reason, Paul's list of objectives for participation would seem more useful (Moser, 1989b). Paul's fivefold objective is presented in a continuum from project efficiency to empowerment. It consists of:

(a) Project efficiency: This can be achieved by using participation to promote agreement, cooperation and interaction among beneficiaries, and between them and the implementing agency of the project. In this way, delays are reduced, a smooth flow of project services is achieved, and overall costs are minimised.

(b) Cost sharing: When cost sharing is the objective of participation, it is done by contributing labour and money to maintain the project.

(c) Effectiveness: Participation tends to enhance project effectiveness when the involvement of beneficiaries contributes to a better project design and implementation and leads to a better match of project services with beneficiary needs and constraints.

(d) Building beneficiary capacity: Beneficiaries may share in the management tasks and may play an active role in monitoring.

(e) Empowerment: The objective of participation creates an equitable sharing of power, political awareness and strengths.

This continuum of objectives can be analysed by using the terms 'means' and 'end'. While the first three objectives can be categorised as a means, the others could be defined as an end. Oakley and Marsden use the terms 'means' and 'end' to distinguish between community participation as a process and as a static action. When identified as an end, it is a process whereby the outcome is empowering, and usually there is a need for a structural change to achieve it.

Paul does not elaborate upon whether empowerment is strictly limited to practical empowerment within the project's activities, or whether it can be extended beyond the project itself to include empowering of a more political nature, which can result in violation and confrontation. Moser (1989b) and Oakley and Marsden (1984) are more explicit about the political nature of participation whose objective is empowerment. Participation is seen as a process of empowering in terms of access to, and control of, the resources necessary to protect livelihood:

> "meaningful participation is concerned with achieving power: the power to influence the decisions that affect one's livelihood."
>
> (Oakley and Marsden, 1984, p. 27)

Midgley (1986) defines the objectives of participation in the context of people's own experience in the decision-making process, which contributes to a higher sense of community and raises the level of social and political consciousness. Actually, this is the assumption underlying some of the World Bank and the USAID projects. They assume that an increase of women's economic participation in development links efficiency and equity together (Moser, 1989b).

2.3.3. When participation?

The real objectives of participation are sometimes more clearly identified if the analysis of 'when participation' is introduced, in terms of the different stages involved in programmes or projects. These stages are identified as: decision-making, planning and implementation.

> "Community participation at the outset, in decision-making, is a precondition if the objective is empowerment. Where participation is a means to achieve a development objective it is usually included only at the implementation and maintenance level."
>
> (Moser, 1989b, p. 85)

As will be seen later, this distinction is not always so clear. For example, the nature of participation of the Bedouin in the project depended more on stages in negotiation and the power that the Bedouin had rather than the mere stages of project.

2.3.4. Whose participation? and how participation?

The extent to which participation really is 'community' participation depends on issues such as who is participating and how participation is initiated.

It is a very common tendency to deal with the community as a homogeneous group and to assume that the process of participation means participation of the whole community through its representatives. Conyers identifies the question of what is a community and who should actually be involved in the planning process (Conyers, 1982) as a general problem of planners. Besides suggesting various criteria to define community, like geographical components, common characteristics and the 'basic harmony' that community usually have, Conyers raises several constraints in identifying community structures, such as the heterogeneity of most communities, and maintains that the constraint of 'how participation' should be incorporated in development projects. This constraint is also mentioned by Skinner (1983a). A lack of experience in this area results in a lack of knowledge of how to incorporate participation in plans. Also the nature of the government concerned is a crucial factor. If the government sees participation as a threatening factor to its political control it can restrict it or eliminate it completely (Skinner, 1983b).

The question of 'whose participation' is also raised by Hollesteiner (1977). She mentions that some modes of participation include only local elites, educated 'solid citizens', while the 'grass roots' sector plays only a minor, if any, role in participation. This is true also for local leaders who take the lead in bringing governments' programmes to the 'grass roots' level, 'interpreting' for the people what has to be done and how it should be done. The 'grass roots' citizens, again, find themselves far removed from the decision-making process. This situation applies particularly to minority groups within the community: women, elderly people, children, and ethnic minorities within the society at large.

Pearse and Steifel (1980) also point out the fact that the form and characteristics of leadership in communities determines the nature of the participation of their people. Leadership in a participatory movement is sometimes embodied in a single individual who has acquired this role through traditional status or by democratic election, or because his personal charisma suits the nature of the movement.

2.3.5. Intensity and instruments of community participation

Intensity refers to the manner in which participation is accomplished. Paul distinguishes four levels of intensity:

(1) Information sharing: with beneficiaries in order to facilitate collective or individual action.

(2) Consultation: when beneficiaries are not only informed but consulted. Beneficiaries have opportunities to interact and provide feedback to the project agency, which can be taken into account at the design and implementation stage.

(3) Decision-making: beneficiaries have a decision-making role in matters of project design and implementation. Oakley and Marsden consider the decision-making process as crucial for real community participation when the objective is empowerment, but at the same time they are very sceptical as to the feasibility of its implementation because:

"A real decision-making process would require a radical change to existing bureaucratic structures and planning procedures. Only this process will lead to empowerment."
(Oakley and Marsden, 1984, p. 21)

(4) Initiation action: this refers to a protective capacity and the confidence to get going on one's own. In using initiation action, the intensity of community participation may be said to have reached its peak, as the beneficiaries are able to take the initiative in terms of actions or decisions pertaining to a project.

The degree to which these levels of intensity are implemented depends largely upon the instruments of implementing participation. By 'instrument' it is meant the institutional agencies used to organise and sustain community participation. These agencies vary in their complexity in terms of design and implementation, according to the level of organisation (macro/national or micro/local level) and according to the objectives defined in each project. Paul categorises three types of instruments: fieldworkers, community workers, and user groups, through which the process of participation of beneficiaries would take place. These instruments are defined variously in different sources as a local decision-making body, local government, or a local development council and were seen as the means to encourage local participation especially in the colonial period (Conyers, 1982).

Objectives, intensity and instruments of community participation are inter-related (Paul, 1986). The same is true of the issues of why, when, whose and how participation. The more complex the objectives of community participation, the greater the need of beneficiary involvement of a high level of intensity, and of powerful instruments. What is highlighted by Paul is the need to search for more sophisticated and internally consistent combinations, as more complex objectives of community participation are attempted. Objectives differ not in terms of the exclusive use of one instrument or level of intensity, but in the combination of instruments and the number of levels of intensity they deploy.

In sum, this chapter has outlined the essential components of operational frameworks which incorporate pluralism, needs and participation into development planning. Its conceptual rationale provides a basis for the identification of ethnic and citizen needs, which together creates the components of pluralist needs, and can be used in the context of discrimination as presented in the next chapter.

CHAPTER 3

Interests and Needs of Ethnic Groups in Settlement Planning under Principles of Pluralism

3.1. THE CONCEPT OF ETHNIC AND CITIZEN NEEDS

Part 3 focuses on the formulation of an operational framework for ethnic groups in striving towards cultural and political pluralism. While the concept of ethnicity and pluralism is increasingly recognised and used in development projects in Western and Third World countries, this awareness of 'ethnicity and development' has not necessarily resulted in translation into planning practice. A growing recognition of concepts of ethnicity stems from the simple truth that almost all countries in the world are ethnically heterogeneous. The recognition of their pluralistic structure goes together with a shift from the 'melting pot' concept which was popular in the United States in the mid-1960s to a more flexible model of pluralist life. For many practitioners involved in different aspects of socio-economic development planning, the lack of an adequate operational framework for dealing with diverse ethnicity has been particularly problematical. The aim of this part is to contribute to the formulation of a framework which, it is hoped, will facilitate the tackling of development from a more pluralistic viewpoint. This framework suggests specific sets of tools which take into consideration the process of social change that ethnic groups experience. It also takes into account the political position of ethnic groups in a situation of pluralism, which is crucial in determining their basic needs — ethnic and citizen needs.

The situation of Bedouin society in Israel, as former nomads living in a modern Jewish state, provides an example of an ethnic group whose ethnicity has been largely ignored in the context of Israel's cultural pluralism, and the methodological tools serve to show this oversight. These methodological tools have generic nature. They can be used in any situation where ethnic groups are involved in a planning process.

3.1.1. The definition of ethnic and citizen needs

The different definitions of pluralism indicate the complexity involved in formulating a planning approach for ethnic groups living in a situation of cultural and political pluralism. One of the difficulties of formulating such a planning approach derives from the different identities applicable to ethnic groups. Ethnic groups can possess a number of identities, but, for the purpose of formulating this new conceptual framework, two distinctive identities were identified.

The dual identity of ethnic groups consists of citizen identity on the one hand and ethnic identity on the other. The combination of the two creates a citizen identity where the ethnic group expects to be granted rights equal to the rest of the citizens in the state. At the same time ethnic groups should be allowed to retain their unique cultural, religious, national or racial heritage, i.e. their ethnic identity. Ethnic identity can be formulated by various components (Prazanska, 1991): territories, historical common memories, clear group boundaries, own political culture, shared culture, way of life. These components define the common interests of ethnic groups. Prazanska argues that the expression of these interests reflect the attempt of ethnic communities to achieve the optimal conditions for their existence.

Therefore, ethnic groups' identity interests can be viewed as their prioritised concerns. After identifying prioritised concerns it is possible to translate them into planning needs, i.e. the means by which these concerns may be addressed, and thereby to formulate policies and planning frameworks (Moser, 1989a).

Citizen identity interests are intended here to be labelled in planning terms as citizen needs. Cultural, religious, ethnic, national and racial identity interests or, in short, ethnic interests, are to be labelled here in planning terms as ethnic needs. Ethnic identity emphasises the uniqueness of ethnic groups, while citizen identity emphasises their similarity or equality. This contrast represents the complexity of formulating a planning approach for ethnic groups. This is displayed in Table 1.

TABLE 1. Identity interests and planning needs

Identity interests	Planning needs	Characteristics
Cultural, traditional, religious, national, racial identity	Ethnic needs	Uniqueness
Citizen identity	Citizen needs	Equality and similarities

This duality of identities is also mentioned by Joo (1991). In a survey carried out in the Slovene inhabited southwestern area of Hungary and the northern border zone of Slovenia inhabited by Hungarians, he discussed the various dimensions of collective identity of these two communities living alongside the Hungarian–Yugoslav border. In the research, the author uses a dual ethnic and civic loyalty in order to avoid, as he puts it, the often ambiguous and controversial term, "national".

Similar concepts are presented in Goldberg and Geers' article on 'Ethnicity and Assimilation in the American Society' (1990). They view ethnicity in the context of immigration position in America. They argue that the ethnic immigrant should become ethnic Americans through the integration of their natural cultural history and close contact between ethnic communities and not through enforced Americanisation. In other words, through the process of assimilation and acculturation or a process of social change, ethnic needs would be met side by side with citizen needs.

Gordon (1964) presents an unconventional approach as related to ethnicity, when mentioning the survival of ethnicity in the face of apparent cultural assimilation. In his policy recommendations he specifies that programmes should acculturate immigrants but not undermine pride in heritage and family bonds. Here again ethnic identity is mentioned in one breath with citizen identity.

While Joo, Goldberg and Geers, and Gordon use ethnic and civic identity to analyse minorities and immigrants positions in societies, the use here of ethnic and citizen needs is for establishing parameters for planning for ethnic groups. In the next section, this use of ethnic and citizen needs in settlement planning is further elaborated.

3.2. SETTLEMENT PLANNING ADDRESSING THE ETHNIC AND CITIZEN NEEDS

The most relevant ethnic and citizen needs within the scope of settlement planning are those that have spatial expression. This means, those needs whose translation into planning is expressed in scaled mapping. If we take the Bedouin society in Israel, ethnic identity interests of the Bedouin can be identified as those which retain their cultural or national identity. In planning terms, spatial expression relates, for example, to meeting their landownership needs, respecting the privacy of the Bedouin clan, especially at the level of the nuclear and extended family, and the privacy of women in the planning process. These can be found in the spatial characteristics of the spontaneous Bedouin settlement, which is largely analysed in the next section.

Citizen identity interests of ethnic groups can be identified as those which provide the opportunity for these groups to be treated as equal citizens. This definition, of course, has many implications for the political power of ethnic groups and their equal integration within the economic, political and social activities of the society at large. In this monograph the spatial expressions of the Bedouin's citizen needs in the planning process intend to include equal employment opportunities, and the implementation of such plans which create jobs in the industrial and the commercial sectors. Another spatial expression of citizen needs is equal access to modern services and infrastructures like education, health, water supply, electricity and roads. These are needs that should be provided equally by the state to all its citizens. These are actually 'basic needs' but here the emphasis is put not only on providing services but distributing them equally.

The planning approach which is formulated to meet the needs of ethnic groups seeks to take into account the dual identity of such groups. This identity, which is different and sometimes contradictory to the identity of the rest of society, calls for different planning needs. The unique use of ethnic and citizen needs as it is presented in this monograph is the ability of these tools to define discrimination in settlement planning within a context of a conflict between minorities and majorities. This is in contrast to Joo (1991) who deals with ethnic groups which are in a process of normalisation with the majority, and the latter tend to accept the minorities in their linguistic and cultural identities. The situation of the Bedouin in Israel is different. They are in a conflict with the state, facing discrimination in planning and development, and therefore the tools developed here are more elaborated in the sense that not only ethnic and citizen needs are formulated but they are used to define discrimination.

In Israel, this approach is useful to each of the ethnic groups which has experienced a process of transition and social change which has possessed different, or contradictory, interests from the society at large, for example, the Oriental Jews, the Ethiopian Jews or the Bedouin. The relationships of these ethnic groups to the majority of society can be defined either in plural or in pluralistic contexts. Some of the Oriental Jews live in a situation of socio-economic conflict with the establishment. Nevertheless, they identify themselves with the majority of the Jewish population in Israel. Their relationship can be analysed from a pluralistic viewpoint. They are in conflict, on socio-economic grounds, but they are part of the majority. The Bedouin, however, as non-Jews, live in a situation of socio-economic and political conflict with the establishment. Their relationship with the establishment is analysed as a conflict in the context of a plural society.

3.3. DISCRIMINATION IN SETTLEMENT PLANNING IN THE CONTEXT OF ETHNIC AND CITIZEN NEEDS

3.3.1. *Ethnic and citizen needs as tools for evaluation of policies and plans*

Once the methodological tools have been established, it is necessary to put ethnic and citizen needs within an appropriate operational framework, so that they can become tools for evaluating policies and plans. The combination of both ethnic and citizen needs as methodological tools to evaluate policies and plans is defined in this monograph as the pluralist needs of such groups. The definition of pluralist needs that I pose in this monograph is that they are met only when both ethnic and citizen needs are met. Then, the policy or plan is a pluralist policy or a pluralist plan. When a policy or plan satisfies only one set of needs, either ethnic or citizen, then I call the policy or plan a uniplan; either citizen uniplan or ethnic uniplan. This new term of the pluralist needs of ethnic groups will be emphasised in the next section, defining discrimination in planning.

An example of the use of different sets of needs as methodological tools to evaluate policies and plans is in the study of gender planning. In gender planning two sets of needs are also formulated which take into account the fact that women and men often have different interests and planning needs in society. It stresses the necessity to distinguish between their separate interests on a gender basis when identifying and translating them into planning needs.

Gender needs are defined as strategic and practical gender needs. Strategic gender needs are those needs which are formulated from the analysis of women's subordination to men. These needs consist of arrangements which provide for a more equal relationship between men and women (Moser, 1989a). This may include the abolition of the sexual division of labour, the alleviation of the burden of domestic labour and childcare, and the removal of institutional forms of discrimination (Molyneux, 1985). Practical gender needs are those that arise from the concrete conditions women experience in their engendered position within the sexual division of labour (Moser, 1989a). They relate to the inadequacies in living conditions which women face in daily life. While practical gender needs are defined by the women themselves, strategic gender needs are most likely to be defined by external interventions (Moser, 1989a).

The rationale behind identifying the two sets of needs in gender planning is in clarifying the different sets of needs which are essential to determining realistic parameters for planning and in indicating the limitations of different policy interventions (Moser, 1989a).

The reason for using the two sets of needs in gender planning relates to the question of whether various interests or needs can be met within an existing political context. The purpose of the determination of practical and strategic gender needs is to clarify the purposes of plans, and their limitations in terms of meeting the needs of women.

The methodological tools of ethnic and citizen needs serve the same purpose, i.e. to establish parameters for plans which would meet the needs of ethnic groups and clarify the plans' limitations within an existing political context. This similar approach to policies and plan evaluation derives from the similarities between gender relationships and ethnic relationships. In both cases — men/women relations and the relationship between ethnic groups and the majority of society — the needs of each of the social groups are different. In both cases the needs of men and the majority of society are usually 'taken into account' within planning schemes, whereas the needs of women and ethnic groups are not always perceived as different and therefore are not always taken into account. In gender relations, this is a result of women's subordination to men. In ethnic relations, this is expressed in the discrimination towards ethnic minorities by the majority of society.

3.3.2. The concept of discrimination in settlement planning

Ethnic groups' dual needs of equality, on the one hand, and of a unique identity, on the other, can lead in fact to discrimination.

The discrimination against ethnic groups becomes apparent when looking at their pluralist needs. I have chosen to employ one of the definitions of discrimination that is used in discussing principles of equality in European Common Market Economic Law. The concept of equality and uniqueness appears in European Community dealings, as the EEC tries to reach equality between its members, while each of them have their own unique political, social and economic system. Here I am using Jacque's definition of discrimination. According to his interpretation discrimination occurs:

> "Either in a *different* treatment of *similar* situations, or in the *similar* treatment of *different* situations."
>
> (Jacque, 1985, p. 139)

This is a rather simplistic definition of discrimination, and it must be noted that discrimination differs according to the context in which it appears. Nevertheless, this definition facilitates the understanding of discrimination against ethnic groups in the context of their pluralist needs.

Discrimination occurs when ethnic groups are treated *differently* from the majority in *similar* situations, i.e. their citizen needs of equality are not met. Discrimination also occurs when ethnic groups are treated *similarly* in *different* situations: when their unique ethnic needs are not taken into consideration in policies and planning schemes, and, in spite of their unique needs, they are treated *similarly* to the rest of society.

Relating the concept of discrimination to the Bedouin settlements, an example of the first type of discrimination is apparent where the Bedouin get *different* types of development of services and infrastructure or *different* access to jobs when compared with the rest of society, in spite of being *equal* citizens of the state.

An example of the second type of discrimination is the fact that planning approaches to Bedouin settlements appear to be *similar* to those of Jewish settlements in spite of the Bedouin's *different* landownership needs, which grew from their *different* ethnic identity as compared to the majority of Jewish people, who do not own land. The same relates to their unique need to protect the privacy of clans and the privacy of women. In order not to be discriminated against, the Bedouin landownership needs and other social needs should be considered in a different settlement planning context.

Pluralist needs are met only when both the following conditions exist:

(i) When citizen needs are met, i.e. when ethnic groups get *similar* treatment in *similar* situations. This answers the principle of equality, as this similar treatment is based on planning principles which emerge from the analysis of the meanings of equality in each society. In the planning of Bedouin settlements this means equality in providing infrastructure and equal employment opportunities.

(ii) When ethnic needs are met, i.e. when ethnic groups get *different* treatment in *different* situations. This answers the principle of uniqueness. This relates to the unique and different needs of ethnic societies, such as landownership needs in the Bedouin case, or privacy of clans and women. Only when this combination exists are they not discriminated against and their pluralist needs are met.

The Bedouin experience of discrimination in employment and provision of infrastructure is a useful indicator when comparing their situation to similar situations for other citizens in the State — those in the rural Jewish settlements. The Bedouin's citizen needs in these two areas require clear spatial expression, which settlement plans have to take into account, and they can be used as clear illustrations of citizen needs in this discussion.

With this new interpretation, a useful tool is provided for establishing parameters to evaluate the real limitations of policies and plans and also to evaluate whether failure of policies and plans results purely from discrimination or just from a lack of awareness of the society's pluralist needs.

While this definition clearly illustrates the complexities of incorporating 'pluralism, ethnicity and development', I intend to examine the argument that meeting pluralist needs in policies and plans would help to prevent discrimination. Thus, an investigation of the record of Israeli government policy regarding Bedouin settlements will be made to show the results of the lack of sensitivity towards, not to mention discrimination against, the ethnic and citizen needs of the Bedouin.

3.3.3. *An evaluation of the spatial characteristics of the spontaneous and planned settlements in the context of Bedouin pluralist needs*

In order to discover whether Bedouin pluralist needs were being addressed by the planners of settlements, the spatial characteristics answering these needs should first be identified. Although this is not an easy task, since the needs themselves were undergoing change because Bedouin society is in a continuing process of transition, nevertheless it at least serves as a starting point for the creation of parameters for evaluating policies and plans. Defining the difference between ethnic and citizen needs also serves to highlight where discrimination occurs. Identification of these two sets of needs is useful in establishing whether plans made for the Bedouin were pluralist plans or merely uniplans which concerned themselves solely with ethnic or citizen needs in isolation.

The identification of Bedouin ethnic needs in settlement planning would also have to be based on the recognition that the spontaneous settlement was a spatial expression of their ethnic needs and could be an example of an ethnic 'uniplan', a 'bottom up' initiation formulated by the Bedouin themselves and to be drawn upon by the planners.

The ethnic and citizen needs of the Bedouin will be examined here based on the patterns of their spontaneous settlements in relation to economic requirements of a dual economy, landownership traditions, social patterns, housing, infrastructure and social services. A comprehensive encompassing of all these elements would serve to give direction to the formulation of plans aimed at meeting Bedouin pluralist needs. How far these needs were met will be examined later in this chapter, in the section dealing with the implementation of the first two planned settlements: Tel Sheva and Rahat.

The Bedouin dual economy and their needs

The Bedouin dual economy refers to the two separate economies which have been created with both traditional and outside wage-earning work. The traditional Bedouin economic activities of agriculture and animal raising necessitate location near water resources and arable land. These two requirements are of primary significance in desert conditions of extreme heat and scarcity of water and fertile land. The spontaneous settlements, therefore, were located near water wells and not far from arable land. When nomadism was at its height, most settlements were located on hill slopes during the winter months, in order to get the maximum protection from the wind and rainstorms, and on the top of hills in the summer to get the benefit of the Brize wind coming from the sea.

Traditional economic needs have changed. As most Bedouin no longer work in agriculture as a sole means of income, the dependency on water and arable land has of course been reduced. Nevertheless, the dual Bedouin economy which still exists gives importance to arable land for agriculture. The Bedouin in general have continued with their traditional economy but at the same time have managed to integrate into the Israeli Jewish labour market. Two separate economies have been created which complemented each other, with both traditional and outside wage-earning work. This is mainly because outside employment is never permanent. Bedouin accept work outside without knowing the duration of their employment. The traditional economy, based on agriculture and animal raising, is a source of economic security (Marx, 1980, p. 2). This applies more to the 'real' Bedouin. For the Fellahin, especially the non-landowners, dual economy is not relevant and they rely mostly on wage-earning work. The fact that the Bedouin are an ethnic minority further perpetuates these two economies, which protects them to some degree from the problem of work discrimination. The traditional economy provides a sense of security and stability. It prevents the Bedouin's total dependency on the uncertain wage-earning work. Wage work assures an improved income and financial capability to purchase more technical equipment to improve their relatively low standard of living. The Bedouin dual economy emphasises the argument that if citizen needs are not met, ethnic needs would be retained as a defense against this type of discrimination. This argument is further elaborated in the next section.

Any settlements planned for the Bedouin has to meet the needs of a dual economy: on the one hand maintaining their agricultural income, for their security, by providing them small plots of land. On the other hand, moving towards new economic activities, particularly among a younger generation, asking that they be treated as equal citizens in the State, requiring of any plans a new, modified spatial expression. In planning terms, the provision of agricultural ground was needed alongside an area for the creation of private enterprises that could be developed within the settlements, in order to develop an independent Bedouin economy and to meet their desire for equal access to jobs in the Jewish economic market. This, of course, required not only physical planning, but also the provision of incentives, subsidies and other financial support similar to that provided to Jewish settlements.

With these two economic activities of agriculture and private enterprise provided for within the layout of a planned settlement, a new dynamic is created. The more citizen needs are met, the less powerful is the expression of ethnic needs as a tool protesting discrimination. Thus it can be assumed that the more Bedouin become involved independently in the Israeli economic market, the less they will be reliant on agriculture. Such a thriving community would always be more able to change.

Landownership needs

The landownership conflict between the authorities and the Bedouin had a marked effect on the ultimate spatial character of spontaneous settlements and the success or failure of Bedouin settlements (Marx and Shela, 1979). The vital need of the land by both peoples, Jewish and Bedouin, resulted in this conflict. As in most clashes over land between governing authorities and ethnic communities, two separate viewpoints come into play: the laws created by states to assure their control over the land and the traditional rules of landownership invoked by the ethnic groups. States customarily use a claim, which also appears in the relevant literature, that nomads by definition do not own land, since they are not territorial because they wander from one place to another as a mechanism to cope with territorial conflicts. However, the more sedentarised they are, the more territorial they become (Rapoport, 1978; Bar, 1989). The Israeli authorities use the 1858 Ottoman Land Law to claim that most Negev lands are state land as they are arable, and according to this law arable land is state land. In contrast to this approach, the Bedouin firmly maintain the right to call their lands their own. Furthermore, they do not consider legal documents as proof of ownership. They claim ownership of land over which they allege to have had longstanding, uninterrupted occupancy, regardless of the fact that they do not hold official documents (Kushan) to prove it (Marx, 1967). As a result of the landownership conflict, spontaneous settlements became dispersed over a large area of 1.5 million dunam in approximately one hundred spontaneous settlements, with over 5000 dwellings (Marx and Shela, 1979). Because of these settlements, this area was not available for use by the state.

Landownership had spatial implications in the location and structure of the spontaneous settlements (Ben David, 1976; Marx and Shela, 1979; Tahal, 1982; Kliot and Medzini, 1985). Settlements developed by landowners tend to be small hamlets with permanent structures, located according to family landownership rights. Non-landowners like the Fellahin and relocated Bedouin, concentrate in large settlements with many tents or other temporary dwellings. Traditionally, the Bedouin will not settle permanently on land that is not their own (Boneh, 1982; Shmueli, 1980). The tradition of the 'real' Bedouin to separate themselves from the Fellahin creates the need for substantial physical distance between the two groups' various settlements.

The location of alternative, planned settlements would have to take into account the traditional rule not to settle on land belonging to other Bedouin. Only appropriate location and a suitable amount of compensation for land that the Bedouin might have agreed to give up would allow them to adapt more easily to a new way of life in a planned settlement.

Meeting the ethnic needs of landowners in such a settlement would signify the state's recognition of Bedouin claims. It would involve treating them *differently* in a *different* situation. They were, anyway, in a different situation as compared to the Jewish majority in terms of landownership, because most Jews do not own land (93% of the land in Israel is state-owned). But being an ethnic minority, their sense of inferiority only had the effect of making them more tenacious in expressing their landownership needs, knowing that they could not integrate on equal terms in other ways within the majority society. The landownership issue became a rallying point by which the Bedouin found a way to call attention to and obtain at least a partial recognition of their citizen needs. If they had been integrated equally into the economic market, perhaps the importance given to the land issue would have disappeared in time. In the existing situation, where they are not treated equally and their ownership claims are still crucial to them, these claims have to be taken into consideration in the settlement planning process.

A solution to the landownership conflict is of paramount importance to the Bedouin. They view the two issues of removal into planned settlements and a government response to their landownership claims as highly connected (Y. Abu Rebeha, 24.8.1988; A. Abu Rebeha, 17.8.1988). They argue that one of the major factors preventing them from moving into the planned settlements is this problem of ownership. It is also the reason, as we have seen, why the great majority of those who have moved to the planned settlements are non-landowners, mostly Fellahin.

Social needs

Traditional social needs also inevitably influenced the spatial nature of the spontaneous settlement. This structure had to honour the necessity of seclusion of the Bedouin clans, especially at the level of the nuclear and extended family. This particularly involved respecting the privacy of the Bedouin women. Accordingly two tendencies characterised the spontaneous settlement: first, a spontaneous settlement was always a gathering of extended families in a sub-tribe or Ruba; second, the Bedouin settlements were of necessity very spacious in order to preserve the privacy of each family. The distances among family dwellings are relatively small, but larger between the different extended families or Rubas in order to limit the chances of undesirable meetings (Ben David, 1976).

The inevitable expansion of the Bedouin family with the birth of new generations is another social need which is met by the space appropriated within the spontaneous settlement. Its ability to expand is an essential part of the settlement's evolution. Amiran *et al.* (1979) identified five stages in the chronological development of a spontaneous settlement influenced by the life cycle of a nuclear family. First, the nuclear family dwelling, usually the tent, is constructed. At this stage, it is one single unit. The next stage occurs when the first son gets married and then another permanent unit, usually a wooden shack, is added. The third stage comes with the son's making of his own family, when he builds a new block dwelling and the wooden shack becomes a kitchen. At the fourth stage, another permanent dwelling for another married son is built. At the last stage the head of the family, too old to live on his own, moves in to live with one of his sons and his previous dwelling, usually the tent, disappears. This description emphasises the need for the family members to live close to one another so as to preserve their respective social roles, and also points to the need for space for the natural growth of the family. These traditional patterns are of course dynamic and might change in the future. But clearly, such different social needs would be expressed in the internal layout of any modern planned settlement.

Bedouin needs in housing

The spontaneous settlement usually consists of assorted kinds of homes varying from tents to block dwellings. The internal structure of the tent reflects the

Bedouin's ethnic needs in housing. The tent is divided into two main parts. The first part is the living area which during the day is occupied by the women who do their domestic work there, cooking, cleaning and embroidering, and where the family members sleep at night. The other part is the guest area or Shigh. It is completely separated from the first to preserve the women's privacy. Since hospitality is one of the important elements of Bedouin tradition, this area is always large and comfortable (Havakuk, 1983). Women can enter this part only when family members are sitting there alone. In order to assure the privacy of the women this part is always located on the northern side and the living part always on the southern side. Guests directly enter the guest area from the east side to avoid unexpected encounters. This pattern has been rigorously adopted in the structure of the permanent dwellings constructed by the Bedouin whether wooden or block structures. They consist of two or three rooms built in a row following the layout of the traditional tent. Different units may be added to the basic structure, like a kitchen or pens for animals.

Today some of this pattern has been adapted for modern houses built by the Bedouin themselves in the planned Bedouin settlements of Aruar and Kessifa. However, the adjustment was still quite traumatic for a Bedouin household, both in terms of adjustment to living in modern houses and the difficulties of daily life. Perhaps a clearer view of the process of transition which the Bedouin had to undergo can be provided by describing one household in Kessifa which I visited during my field work in 1988. This was the family of a young Fellahin who had two wives and eight children. Each of the wives lived in a separate stone house. The man himself lived with his first wife in a relatively large house. His second wife lived nearby in a smaller, rather modest house. His house was located at the end of a cul-de-sac in a corner plot. He and his family were living on only one floor, the second floor being unfinished. There were two bedrooms, two guest-rooms, a dining room, kitchen, toilet and bathroom. The larger guest-room was located in front of the house. It had many windows and was furnished in traditional oriental style with carpets and cushions on the floor. Guests enter this room through a separate entrance so that the privacy of women is respected. The other guest-room, without a separate entrance, was furnished in western style with sofa and armchairs and even air conditioning. In one bedroom, mattresses were kept in the corner of the room, and at night they were spread on the floor for the children to sleep on.The other bedroom had a modern double bed and a large closet.

The kitchen had modern facilities like refrigerator, oven and gas fire. There was a table and chairs in the dining room whereas previously when living in tents and even in their spontaneous settlements the Bedouin used to eat seated on the floor. The modern facilities in the kitchen were a problem at early stages of the evacuation, and five years after the evacuation to the settlement, the Bedouin women were still not accustomed to using these facilities, and I saw some of them still cooking on a fire outside in the yard while their modern ovens remained unused. The toilet and bathroom were modern but unfinished. As there was no central sewage system, the Bedouin used sewage pits. The use of toilets was also a problem for them when they first moved in because the Bedouin considered it unrespectable to relieve themselves so close to the place they actually live. Previously they would walk a long distance for this purpose. In the planned settlement this was of course impossible and they had to get used to modern toilets. This description clearly emphasises the results of lack of adequacy to Bedouin ethnic needs in housing in existing plans. Although the houses were built by the Bedouin themselves, the plans were not suited to the process of transition which the Bedouin society was experiencing. Bedouin pluralist needs in housing in a planned settlement would require not only the gathering of the right to build houses according to their own traditions but also the completion of the construction of such houses so that a better transition to living in permanent houses is possible. As to how the government addressed these needs, the clearest examples in Israel of public housing provided by the state which has not met pluralist needs are those of the Oriental Jews in the development towns during the 1950s and the houses built for the Bedouin by the government in Tel Sheva in 1965. These latter proved totally unsuitable, especially when it came to the privacy of women and land constraints, and they therefore were a complete failure (see next section). In the two planned settlements of Aruar and Kessifa the government indeed permitted the Bedouin to build their own houses but here there was not enough guidance as to the optimal size of the house that would enable the owners to finish it with their resources, and this created the undesirable result that most houses in Aruar and Kessifa were not finished.

Infrastructure and social services

Because of its dispersed area, even nowadays the spontaneous settlement has no basic services like water supply, electricity, sewage system, or social and commercial services. Water is brought by tanks, and electricity, if provided, is supplied by private generators. In central locations the government build schools and health clinics to serve the nearest settlements. But the schools are located sporadically over a large distance, which does not encourage or facilitate the participation of children in school activities.

The living conditions in a spontaneous settlement were beautifully described by a Jewish woman, a social worker, who has been living with the Bedouin for several years:

"When they gave them a tap they decided to pass the pipe under the road. That was ten or twelve years ago and they connected it to their houses, and if they were taken to jail, they got taken to jail (because it wasn't legal). They didn't go to jail, and I

have water. But I have many hours without water, because the pressure is weak and
the pipe is very thin, so at certain times when they are using water down below, I
have no water up on the hill."

In planned settlements infrastructure services are basic components in raising
the standard of daily life as well as in aiding the integration of the Bedouin into
the Israeli economy. They should include, as well as the above provision of water,
roads, telephone communication, and social services such as education and health
institutions, and commercial facilities.

The development of education and health services would be a significant step in
meeting the citizen needs of the Bedouin. Education would introduce basic skills
to the young generation for their greater involvement in modern economy.

From rudimentary abilities like literacy and mathematics to technical skills like
carpentry, locksmithy and other technical studies, basic education and training are
needed within the settlement itself to encourage full participation of the Bedouin
children within an education system and to enable them to proceed with higher
education if they wish. Health services would be a further incentive towards the
Bedouin accepting change, and commercial services like shops and banks are
crucial to the economic integration of the Bedouin within the Israeli market.

Such a checklist of pluralist needs in settlement planning can be made for every
ethnic group in a process of transition or social change, where ethnic needs derive
from the traditions, customs, taboos and behaviour of ethnic groups and citizen
needs aim at providing an equal level of infrastructure and access to employment.

Meeting Bedouin pluralist needs in settlement planning and the obstacles to be faced

Meeting pluralist needs in settlement planning would mean combining both
ethnic and citizen needs in addressing each of the issues discussed. In the first
attempts by the Israeli authorities to shape the structure of the settlements, during
the period 1973–1979, two types of approach were taken. The first projected an
extension of the spontaneous settlement and can be considered an ethnic 'uniplan'
with little support for citizen needs. The second was the planned settlement, which
was unfortunately little more than a citizen uniplan in emphasising provision of
infrastructure and services at the expense of the society's ethnic needs.

What the Bedouin really wished for was legal recognition of their spontaneous
settlements and subsequent provision of infrastructure and services. If the
spontaneous settlements had been given legitimacy and citizen needs provided,
Bedouin pluralist needs in settlement planning would have been met.

The authorities explain why they have not legally recognised the spontaneous
settlements. Such recognition would clash with their objective of development of
the Negev by the Jewish majority. The officials claim that the perpetualising or
legalising of spontaneous settlements would mean occupation of those 1.5 million

dunam of the Negev which has been allocated for other land uses crucial to Jewish aims. The authorities also excused themselves by claiming that the provision of Bedouin citizen needs in their spontaneous settlements would be very costly because of their wide dispersion. As an alternative, the authorities created the first planned settlements. What is necessary now is to analyse to what extent these planned settlements in fact met Bedouin pluralist needs.

3.3.4. *Earlier attempts by the authorities to meet Bedouin needs in the planned settlements*

The regional level of planning

The complexities involved in meeting Bedouin pluralist needs were first seen when determining the number and size of the planned settlements in the formulation of the 1973 Master Plan. This is a very crucial issue since the size of each new settlement affected the total number to be built. The larger the settlement, the smaller the total number of settlements required. The Bedouin preferred as many small settlements as possible, emulating the structure of the spontaneous settlements. The authorities were more interested in concentrating them into only a few large scale sites.

(a) The Bedouin preferences. The Bedouin prefer small sized settlements because this size, they argue, suits the traditional and social needs of tribal or clan segregation. They favour living in communities based on clan or tribal units. They also prefer the agriculture based settlement because they are still attached to agriculture for maintaining their dual economy. As one Bedouin expressed it:

> "the most suitable pattern of settlement which fits our traditional life is the agricultural settlement."
>
> (Y. Abu Rebeha, 1979, p. 33)

The Bedouin took the Israeli Moshav (agricultural cooperative) as an example of the kind of small sized agricultural settlement that they would like to live in:

> "These patterns of agricultural settlements like the Israeli Moshavim will provide us with a higher level of security for me, my son, my brothers and for the next generation ... in this way it will be easier for a Bedouin to give up his land to the state."
>
> (Y. Abu Rebeha, 1979, p. 33)

Thus the Bedouin saw the most favourable resolution of their problems to be the legalisation of spontaneous settlements or, if planned settlements were offered, they would opt for them to be small in size and based on agriculture, so as to meet their pluralist needs of dual economy, landownership and social segregation.

(b) The Israeli authorities' policy. In contrast to Bedouin preferences, the Israeli authorities' policy at the end of the 1950s called for the establishment of only several urban oriented planned settlements, originally nine in number.

Then, because of water scarcity in the Negev, the government decided to develop
only three settlements (Kliot and Medzini, 1985). In 1973, the policy changed
again and it was decided that three more should be added for a total of six
planned settlements. The reason for the additions was mainly the difficulties
the authorities faced in planning the concentration of Bedouin from some one
hundred spontaneous settlements into only three new settlements. It was difficult
to displace tribes who lived far from the proposed sites. It was also impossible
to settle tribes from different social backgrounds in a single site, especially if
those tribes were in permanent conflict (Government of Israel Ministerial
Economic Committee, decision of 30.5.1973). Further changes in approach
led the six planned settlements to grow to seven. It is clear why the authorities
were interested in concentrating the Bedouin in only these seven sites, each with
15,000–25,000 people. It was less costly in terms of its infrastructure and, what
is more important, less land was required than in the construction of a greater
number of small sized settlements.

Officially, the rationale behind these decisions was explained in terms of
employment, the standard of services, social factors and financial constraints
(Kaplan *et al.*, 1979a). From the perspective of employment, it was argued that
only 10% of the Bedouin were employed in agriculture, with the remainder
working in industry, services and construction. In large size settlements, the
employment opportunities would be far more diverse than in a small agriculture
oriented settlement. Even if an agricultural settlement did suit the Bedouin
lifestyle, it would not be possible for the whole Bedouin population to work on
it, because of water scarcity and the lack of soil appropriate for cultivation in the
Negev (U. More, 3.7.1988).

Another argument favouring larger size related to the standard of services. It
was argued that large sized sites ensured a higher standard of services than small
agricultural settlements. Furthermore, from a social standpoint the planners saw
a social advantage in the tribal integration that would take place in large scale
settlements. Agricultural settlements had up till then been inhabited by only
one tribe.

Finally, from the financial perspective, large settlements have the 'advantage of
scale'. This means that while basic services and infrastructure would have to be
provided even for a small population, it is obviously financially expedient to settle
more people together so that the costs per person are reduced.

It is clear that the alternatives chosen for the planned settlement served the
authorities' priorities, but did they also meet Bedouin pluralist needs? There
is something to the argument that large scale settlements promised diversified
employment and the provision of proper services. Yet, these services could not
be supplied to small settlements, as had already been learned in the small scale
Jewish settlements where the level of such services was poor (Marx, 1988). But the

idea of a large settlement went totally against the Bedouin social need for tribal segregation.

In these first plans the landownership issue was meanwhile steadfastly ignored. The basic premise underlying the government's policies was that there was no relationship between the landownership conflict and the planned settlements (Albek, 29.8.1988). This approach was also expressed in the attitude of the planners of Rahat:

> "The landownership issue is no more than a legal issue, whereas the necessity to settle Bedouin derives from the processes of changes which the Bedouin society experiences, and the duty of the state to supply an equal level of services to its citizens which is impossible to implement with the present dispersion of the spontaneous settlements."
>
> (Kaplan *et al.*, 1979, p. 6)

Thus the landownership needs of the Bedouin were not being met in any way. However, unofficially, it was clear that the planners were aware of the connection between landownership and planned settlements, but they chose to discount this, relying on the fact that meanwhile the Fellahin and other non-landowners would be ready to move to these settlements and perhaps believing that the 'real' Bedouin would follow them in time.

The eventual government Master Plan, published in 1973, specified seven planned settlements, optimistically listing the tribes expected to move into each. The location of the settlements was selected, the planners claimed, according to Bedouin preferences (Kaplan *et al.*, 1979a). But this was questionable because at that time the Bedouin were still staunchly refusing to be relocated.

The number and size of the planned settlements mentioned in the state plans clearly represented a citizen uniplan approach, its justification being in terms of provision of modern infrastructure and services to the Bedouin — again ignoring their ethnic needs. The government, however, while neglecting landownership needs, claimed that their social needs were met in the internal layout of the settlements included in the plan.

The local level of planning: internal layout of the first planned settlements

Because the idea of social integration of various tribes within one settlement went against Bedouin custom, this point of conflict was to be addressed by a unique internal layout in the plan, based on clear tribal segregation. The principles guiding the planners would ensure that the physical layout of the settlement would follow the traditional social structures of Bedouin society in the spontaneous settlements. The planners approached the planned settlement adhering to the following hierarchy:

Social structures	Physical structure
Nuclear family	House
Extended family	Alley or cul-de-sac
Ruba or tribe	Neighbourhood
A number of tribes	Settlement

Source: Kaplan and Amit (1979b), p. 4.

The above hierarchy follows the tradition of segregation of tribes or sub-tribes to preserve the privacy of each social unit and minimise inter-tribal friction. At the same time, the planners tried to plan a settlement which would be compact enough to allow it a proper provision of services. Such a contradictory task required compromise: on the one hand the traditional need for privacy within expanse, on the other the practical requirement of relative restriction in order to minimise costs.

This goal was to be achieved in the planning of the neighbourhoods. The neighbourhood was considered by the planners as the basic unit in the hierarchical structure. Each neighbourhood was planned for only a single sub-tribe or Hamula. It was located on a distinctive topographical feature, such as a hill, and at a large distance from its neighbours. Generally, there is no through pathway from one neighbourhood to another, the passage of 'strangers' through the neighbourhood constituting something of an invasion of privacy (Kaplan and Amit, 1979b). The inner structure of the neighbourhood was based on a hierarchical pattern as well, in which a main road circled the entire neighbourhood. From the main road small alleys or cul-de-sacs were constructed for the Hamulas or extended families within the tribe. Building the houses along the cul-de-sac ensured that strangers would not interfere with the privacy of members of the Hamula, especially the women. The usual practice was for the extended families to purchase a number of plots, so as to enable the sons of the family to build their houses alongside the patriarchal house, thereby ensuring the continuity of the clan territory in the same way as in the spontaneous settlement.

The planners designed what they saw as the optimum settlement plan. They created an aggregation of neighbourhoods, similar in their social identity to the spontaneous settlements and respecting the need for seclusion, but where large scale, high quality services were provided for the whole settlement as one entity. The planners also considered the changing needs of the Bedouin by way of planning 'open spaces' between the neighbourhoods. Foreseeable expansion into these spaces would eventually reduce the existing distances between neighbourhoods, and perhaps social segregation could be expected to be of less importance in the future. However, this type of settlement has not proved successful, as we shall see in the cases of Tel Sheva and Rahat, mainly because the basic assumptions of the planners, that the Bedouin's needs would be met, proved to be wrong and because this pattern was still very costly to realise and therefore its infrastructure was only slowly built.

The experiment of planned Bedouin settlements: Tel Sheva and Rahat
(a) Tel Sheva: the first planned Bedouin settlement.

The planning process of Tel Sheva which was realised in 1965 represents a pre-Master Plan approach to planned Bedouin settlements. In fact, the approach adopted in the subsequent Master Plan was based in part on what was learned from the failure of Tel Sheva. It failed despite the fact that it contained the most modern facilities (Kliot and Medzini, 1985; Tahal, 1982).

Several explanations have been offered for the failure, most of them connected with the fact that the spatial pattern of the settlement did not meet the Bedouin's pluralist needs. The settlement was built on land expropriated from resident Bedouin and therefore those from other areas refused to live on it, because they would not reside on land belonging to other tribes. Land compensation was not offered to the landowners who were willing to move to the settlement. This fact discouraged 'real' Bedouin from moving to the settlement, because they feared that purchase of houses in Tel Sheva would nullify their legal rights to lands on which they had ownership claims. This 1965 settlement plan, furthermore, did not allow extended families to reside separately from each other. This created a relatively over-populated neighbourhood in contrast to the widely dispersed spontaneous settlement. The houses were built by the government according to internal designs which also did not meet Bedouin needs. The distribution of the houses was considered too dense, and their proximity was seen as threatening the modesty of the Bedouin women.

There was also an absence of job opportunities within the settlement itself, since workshop areas were not developed. In the end, only Fellahin moved into Tel Sheva and only in small numbers (Tahal, 1982).

In response to these failures, a second plan for Tel Sheva was introduced in 1977, which offered 34 separate residential neighbourhoods with plots of land of one dunam for building homes on (Horner, 1982). But these changes in the physical layout did not induce the Bedouin to move in again mainly because the landownership conflict still remained unsolved.

(b) Rahat: an implementation of the Master Plan approach.

Rahat, the second Bedouin planned settlement, was built in 1973. It was designed according to the principles of internal layout developed in the Master Plan presented earlier in the chapter. The settlement consisted of several neighbourhoods, each of them again separated from the others and identified with different social groups. Schools and health clinics were built in some neighbourhoods. The commercial centre was located at the entrance to the settlement and included shops, a bank and the town council. Rahat had a population of 16,000 in 1989.

In Rahat, as in Tel Sheva, a landownership solution was not part of the settlement planning process. Therefore, most of its residents are Fellahin, although in the last ten years 'real' Bedouin have also joined, after a neighbourhood was built on their land and integrated into the settlement.

The wide dispersion of the settlement caused financial problems at the implementation phase, the construction of a large infrastructure being, as mentioned, so costly. As a result, the sewage system, roads and telephones have not been fully completed. Again there were no employment resources to allow for the creation of jobs within the settlement, so that most Bedouin in Rahat work outside the settlement, in Be'er Sheva. Furthermore, the promise of irrigated agricultural plots to maintain their dual economy was not in fact honoured.

One of the young Bedouin who lives in Rahat expressed his feeling of discrimination:

> "We talk about unkept promises — Rahat is one such example. It is a settlement, not a town, moshav or kibbutz. I call it merely a settlement without any unique significance. Is there any other settlement with 18,000 people without one single employment place except for jobs with the council or in schools? There isn't any other such example, not in this country and not in Africa. There they provide them employment with embroidery. Where else can you find such a big settlement without a sewage system? They say it is expensive. So they have to decide to make sewage systems instead of other less necessary development projects like paths."

The confined area of individual neighbourhoods meant that there was no room for future expansion of the family within neighbourhoods, as was possible in the spontaneous settlement (A. Bar, 4.7.1988). The separate question concerning the feasibility of the eventual integration of different tribes is also highly debatable. Opponents argue that the structure of the tribe and, more than this, the identity of the extended family are still very strong and will not evolve into the planners' assumption of greater social interaction between different tribes.

The planned settlements, intended to diminish spatial conflicts between the Bedouin's ethnic and citizen needs, failed to do so in practice. The Bedouin were discriminated against in both areas. They experienced discrimination, at this stage, in their citizen needs, being offered different, inferior services and infrastructure and different access to jobs in spite of their official status as equal citizens. They suffered discrimination in their ethnic needs, since the implementation of the urban oriented settlement did not take into consideration their dual economic needs with provision of agricultural plots. Finally, by the authorities not including landownership solutions in the settlement planning process, the Bedouin's landownership needs were not met. The sense of discrimination of Bedouin in the settlement planning process further emphasises the importance they put to their ethnic needs as tools against such types of discrimination. This is emphasised mainly in the Bedouin strong claims for land as a security source of living.

However, the balance of ethnic and citizen needs as seen in the next section is not always clear cut. It is more of a dynamic process and depends to a large extent on ethnic groups' sense of economic, political and social security.

3.4. THE BALANCE OF ETHNIC AND CITIZEN NEEDS

The process of identifying the ethnic and citizen needs, as carried out in the previous chapters, assumes in fact that ethnic groups have dual identities. However, it can be argued that they do not always have a dual identity. Moreover, the balance of their needs is constantly changing and depends on whether ethnic groups are discriminated against or totally assimilated. The expression of ethnic needs by ethnic groups in conflict with the authorities, who are carrying out discriminatory policies, can be seen as a way of calling attention to, and obtaining, their citizen needs.[1]

This is indeed the case with the blacks, Mexicans and Puerto Ricans living in the United States, as well as the Oriental Jews and the Bedouin in Israel. The same occurs with immigrants who find themselves in an inferior position when they are not given citizenship in their new countries. Indeed, it might be said that the very conflict itself has given renewed momentum to, and enhanced, the sense of ethnic identity:

> "In general then, people from Italy or Greece become ethnic Italian or ethnic Greek only on leaving Italy and Greece or being children or perhaps even later descendants of immigrants. Ethnicity basically replaces lost national or citizenship affiliation."
>
> (Shelef, 1990, p. 12)

Another example is provided by the United Kingdom, where the real ethnic groups are the immigrant black or Asian groups. Conversely, white immigrants groups from Australia or South Africa are never referred to as ethnic groups (Shelef, 1990).

The experience of the Bedouin in Jordan, and the Australians and Americans in the United Kingdom, lead to the assumption that the more an ethnic group has free and equal access to socio-economic and political resources in the state, i.e. the less it is discriminated against in its citizen needs, the less dominant are ethnic needs.

It is obviously a difficult task to prove which process determines which. Some can argue that because ethnic needs are less dominant, ethnic groups are more exposed to changes, and therefore more involved in the socio-economic and political life of a state. As a result they do not require different treatment in different situations. They are assimilated. Joo (1991) discusses a situation of normalisation of minority–majority relationships. In this case, he argues, the duality of ethnic and citizen affiliation can be short lived, namely, it exists only for a transitional period preceding the complete assimilation of the minority by the majority (linguistic and cultural assimilation). This is true where there is consensus or a sense of collective identity (religious, national, political). Then, indeed, ethnic and civic identities are not conflicting. The balance of ethnic and citizen needs is different when majority–minority relationships are antagonistic as in the case of the Bedouin in Israel. Then the actual conflict is on the contradictory interests of the ethnic and citizen identities of the various ethnic groups.

A clear example of the use of ethnic needs as a tool for obtaining citizen needs or against discrimination is the Bedouin dual economy in Israel. As previously mentioned, the Bedouin in Israel retain their traditional agricultural economy as an economic security against work discrimination. They have maintained their traditional economy but at the same time they have managed to integrate into the Israeli Jewish labour market. Two separate economies have been created which complement each other. This is mainly because outside employment is never permanent. Bedouin accept work outside without knowing the duration of their employment. The traditional economy, based on agriculture and animal raising, therefore functions as a source of economic security (Marx, 1980).

The full economic integration for the Bedouin into the Israeli labour market may diminish the status and value of traditional agriculture and land as a safeguard against economic insecurity and limited access to jobs. This example shows that the balance between ethnic and citizen needs is dynamic and depends on the extent to which ethnic groups are treated equally. If most Bedouin could rely on outside wage work, they would probably leave their traditional lifestyle and traditional economy, as have the Bedouin in Jordan. Most of the Bedouin in Jordan have started to leave their traditional lifestyle and emigrate into urban areas as they become integrated to some extent into the socio-economic and political life of the Jordanian state:

> "While the Bedouin constitute only a small percentage of the total population of Jordan (about 7%) they have continued to play a major role in its affairs. Not the least of their diverse roles is that they have given Jordan a certain attractive image, in addition to the acculturation process whereby many Bedouin customs, traditions and values have filtered throughout Jordanian society."
>
> (Abu Jaber and Gharaibeh, 1980, p. 3)

They are becoming politically, economically and socially integrated into the Jordanian state and therefore retaining their ethnic identity is of less significance for them.

It can be concluded that the balance of the two sets of needs depends upon the type of discrimination against ethnic groups in the state as a whole; if citizen needs are not completely met, i.e. ethnic groups are treated differently in similar cases, then most probably ethnic needs would be kept as a defense against this type of discrimination.

3.4.1. *The balance of ethnic and citizen needs in different class and age groups*

So far the analysis of the balance of ethnic and citizen needs has assumed homogeneity within societies without considering the different social divisions within societies, such as class, gender and age. This monograph highlights the dominant collective influence of ethnicity and therefore stresses particular sets of needs of the different social groups. The question of gender needs and interests, though fascinating and important in its own right, is beyond the scope of this monograph. The different needs of class and age groups and the way they affect settlement planning is emphasised through the example of the negotiation with the Bedouin in the evacuation and resettlement project.

There is a class division within Bedouin society, between 'real' Bedouin and the Fellahin, which strongly illustrates the need for a subtle and sophisticated understanding when dealing with the intricacies of their ethnic and citizen needs. The ethnic needs of the 'real' Bedouin are different from those of the Fellahin, who are considered a lower class among the Bedouin.

The different balances of ethnic and citizen needs influenced the process of negotiation with the Bedouin. This is illustrated in the three case studies which were part of the evacuation and resettlement project; with the Fellahin group — Abu Arar and the 'real' Bedouin tribe-Abu Rebeha and Abu Gueid.

The participation of the Abu Arar Fellahin in the negotiation process:
the significance of class factors

The Fellahin, not being traditional landowners, and having less at stake, are more concerned with meeting their citizen needs, do not retain their ethnic identity, and are more easily integrated into mainstream society. Thus they attain similar status to the 'real' Bedouin, and their class differences blur in the eyes of the state.

The first steps in the negotiation process for the evacuation of the Bedouin from Tel Malhata were very tough because of the strong objection of the 'real' Bedouin. The first meeting started with the Fellahin groups because their ethnic needs were of less importance to them. Their inferiority within Bedouin society will be diminished only when they are considered equal citizens in the eyes of the state. However, they will always remain inferior on ethnic base.

As the first group to negotiate, the Abu Arar Fellahin were in a very strong position in the negotiation process. Once the negotiations started, the unified objections and apparent homogeneity of the Bedouin dissolved, and, having no single voice, their power decreased. The menial class Abu Arar, numbering some 1000, had lived divided between three 'real' Bedouin tribes: the Abu Rebeha,

Abu Gweid and Abu Qrenat. They made land claims over an area of some 10,000 dunam (1000 ha). Most of it (60%) was within the site of the airfield, in the southern part of Tel Malhata, and the rest lay on the proposed site of the planned settlement of Aruar.

The willingness of the Abu Arar to negotiate was, in fact, largely due to the many illegal constructions on their land, which were under constant threat of demolition. This situation had got worse from 1978 and the negotiation with the Implementation Authority served as a convenient way out for them. In moving into a planned settlement they would finally live in legal houses.

The lesser significance attached to the symbolic value of landownership by the Fellahin was another reason why they were more willing to negotiate with the Implementation Authority. Because of the different balance of their ethnic and citizen needs, they were more willing to accept planned settlements than the 'real' Bedouin. But they remained as stubborn as ever in their specific land requirements. They insisted that they would evacuate the area only after a new, third, planned settlement was built on their land in Aruar. This third settlement was not included within the 1980 law, although it was one of the seven planned settlements announced in the Bedouin Master Plan. It satisfied the old Bedouin demand for a settlement for each tribe.

The Abu Arar, setting a new precedent, agreed as part of any bargain to let other tribes settle on its lands within the borders of Aruar. This opened the way to a solution to the planning constraints caused by the custom forbidding Bedouin from settling on land belonging to other Bedouin without their explicit permission. This arrangement would enable the Implementation Authority to evacuate other Bedouin groups and to settle them in Aruar. By obtaining the approval of the Abu Arar landowners to settle other Bedouin in their lands, the Authority sought to reduce other tribes' objections to moving into this settlement. For such an agreement, the Implementation Authority was willing to pay a price, and they set about convincing the decision-makers to build a third planned settlement, beyond the scope of the 1980 law, in Aruar. The Abu Arar then had achieved on their own what every Bedouin tribe had long sought — a new settlement on their own lands.

The powerful position of Abu Arar also meant that they could insist on becoming an independent 'tribe'. Traditionally they had been subordinated to the Abu Rebeha, Abu Gweid and Abu Qrinat tribes, and they wished to unite into a newly formed tribe with a leader who would be formally recognised as a 'sheikh'. But in exchange for their willingness to evacuate and accept other Bedouin in their land, the Abu Arar group made other exceptional demands. They asked for compensation for lands that originally were not included within the site determined by the law. By including them, they got higher remuneration, which enabled them to better adjust to a modern lifestyle. The Implementation Authority was so anxious to reach an agreement, that it not only convinced the politicians to build another town in Aruar, but also persuaded the defense authorities to give up part of their land along the southern boundary of the military airfield so that extra lands formerly belonging to the Abu Arar would now be included within the border of the town. But this was not the end. Its strong motivation to come to an understanding with the Abu Arar led the Implementation Authority to consent to much higher compensation rates, in comparison to the rates demanded by other groups in the area. In these unofficial agreements it granted this and many other concessions involving the planning of the internal layout of the settlement.

We can see that the importance put on citizen needs by the Fellahin made them more open to negotiate with the authorities, and as the first group to negotiate they gained higher compensations than the other groups.

The balance of ethnic and citizen needs as expressed in the participation of the Abu Rebeha 'real' Bedouin in the negotiation process

As mentioned before, the 'real' Bedouin attached greater importance to ethnic needs, like concepts of landownership, because their land assets gave them a sense of superiority over the Fellahin. It is only on ethnic grounds that they are superior.

The 'real' Bedouin's sense of superiority over the Fellahin, their concepts of landownership and the greater importance they attach to ethnic needs, are especially strong among the Abu Rebeha tribe. The Abu Rebeha is the leading Bedouin tribe. Their sheikh was the first Bedouin member in Israeli Parliament. They possess a large area of lands in the Be'er Sheva Valley: 141,619 dunam (18.2%) out of a total of 776,856 dunam (Tahal, 1982). They had occupied these lands for generations without interruption and continued to do so even when most of the Bedouin were concentrated in the reservation area in 1949. The fact that the leader of the tribe was a member of the Knesset also reinforced their position as the leading tribe in the Negev and not merely amongst the tribes in the Tel Malhata area. All this made them more stubborn in holding onto their landownership rights.

The authorities also recognised the Abu Rebeha as the leading tribe because of the large size of its land and because of the good rapport this tribe had with them through its leader. Most of its younger generation were educated: the first medical doctor came from this tribe, others are lawyers, and many work as teachers. So the Abu Rebeha had more prestige and was better accepted by the authorities.

This influencial position made them more determined not to give up their land assets which they regarded as a symbol both of their leadership and their ethnic uniqueness. They wanted to reach a special landownership agreement which would take into account and preserve their superiority. This had to be different from the agreement reached with the Fellahin. They still objected to the Landownership

Law, arguing that it discriminated against them by coupling them with the Fellahin. This view was expressed by the former Advisor to the Prime Minister on Arab Affairs:

> "they did not sign an agreement, (and this was) in order to retain their dignity. If the Abu Rebeha takes the money for his land and moves to his plots (in a planned settlement) how will his dignity be expressed? The dignity of the Bedouin is expressed in the fact that he is a landowner and the Fellahin worked for him as his peasant. If he loses his land all his dignity is gone. Landownership provides him with power also in relating to the authorities."

The Abu Rebeha tribe was directly affected by the evacuation. They claimed ownership of 8514 dunam of the airfield site (13.1% of the total area), 3619 dunam in the planned settlement of Kessifa (33.6% of the total), and another 1000 dunam in the other planned settlement of Aruar (8% of the total) (Tahal, 1984). They also claimed that all the land that the Fellahin handed to the state was originally theirs. As one of the tribe's members says:

> "We are the leading tribe. The land they (the Fellahin) sold to the state was our land. They bought the land from us and then sold it to the Jews."

It was the Sheikh as the chief representative of the Bedouin who helped the authorities to reach agreements with the Fellahin and because of his position as Bedouin representative his tribe therefore felt that they were entitled to better compensation for their own land. The Abu Rebeha tribe aimed to retain the class differences within Bedouin society and to preserve their superiority. To retain their dominance, they wanted a higher level of compensation for lands evacuated by them. This attitude was expressed by one of the young leaders in the tribe:

> "We will not accept the law terms. We are part of this issue unlike the others (Fellahin) who have neither lands nor interests in this issue. We are a leading family that has many lands, we own ten of thousands of dunams in the Be'er Sheva Valley, and we are the leaders in Bedouin landownership claims. We do not agree to accept compensation of 20% of the land. We are willing to compromise. About how much? We will negotiate it in a serious negotiation with the state. In the meantime we strongly refuse to accept the solutions offered by the authorities."

The second issue on which they expected to be treated differently concerned the type of planned settlement offered them. They believed that urban sites were adequate solutions for the Fellahin, but as landowners they demanded an agricultural settlement for each of their two clans (Ben David, 1982). In fact they called for the legitimisation of their two spontaneous settlements, one near the location of Kessifa where the family of the Sheikh lived, the other located north of the airfield site at Hirbeth Kahal, where the other clan, headed by another Sheikh, lived. The Implementation Authority thought that reaching an agreement with the leading tribe would serve as a great catalyst, leading the rest of the Bedouin to agree to moving to the planned settlements. Efforts were therefore made to build at Kessifa to include the Abu Rebeha spontaneous settlement. But, despite earlier promises from the Authority, the second clan at Hirbeth Kahal failed in their bid to keep their own settlement. The Authority wished to assert its position and feared that further recognition of spontaneous settlements would lead to greater intransigence from all the other tribes.

Meanwhile, the Authority was happy to meet the needs of the clan of the Sheikh. The plans for Kessifa, especially its location site, aimed to satisfy their demands by legitimising the spontaneous settlement, including it within a larger planned settlement in an area to be reserved for future development, and thus preserving its isolation by assuring sufficient distance from other groups. The Abu Rebeha could enjoy the benefits of infrastructure and services and also still have power and control over the Fellahin who would move to the planned settlement.

The participation of the Abu Gweid 'real' Bedouin tribe in the negotiations — the introduction of the age factor

The participation of the Abu Gweid 'real' Bedouin represents the entrance of the age factor in the dynamic process of negotiations between the authorities and the Bedouin. Now the younger generation was to have a gradually increasing voice in the process. Having their own particular sets of needs, the younger Bedouin were open to changes and more willing to negotiate, and this was another component which broke the homogeneity of the Bedouin.

The Abu Gweid tribe consists of five clans: the Zeraia, Maabda, Abu Msaad, Abu Gweid and Rahahla. The case of the Abu Gweid clan represented a situation in which 'real' Bedouin were ready to move to the settlement at Aruar, because the balance and nature of their ethnic and citizen needs were different from those of the Abu Rebeha Bedouin.

The Abu Gweid are the second largest tribe among the Zullam group of tribes in terms of landownership. They laid claim to the largest area of land within the airfield site — 17,164 dunam and 26% of the total. In Kessifa they claimed 2997 dunam, which was 27.8%, and in Aruar 3488 dunam, 27.9% of the total area (Tahal, 1984).

Each clan was represented in the negotiations by its own leader, with the Sheikh of the tribe representing only the Abu Gweid clan. The Implementation Authority negotiated with each clan separately. The leader of the Abu Gweid clan was young, and for the younger generation citizen needs took precedence over ethnic needs — the opposite situation to that of the Abu Rebeha tribe. The dominance of the younger generation led to their relatively painless acceptance of the move to a planned settlement, in similar fashion to the Fellahin groups, since their pluralist needs were more easily met.

But age rather than class was the determining factor here. The old Abu Gweid Sheikh had refused to talk with the Implementation Authority about evacuation in the early stages of the negotiations. In fact he demanded a change in the airfield boundaries so that his lands would not be included in the area expropriated. The Implementation Authority did change the boundaries somewhat, but not enough to leave untouched all of the tribe's lands. The old Sheikh remained stubborn and for him protecting these lands was the most important aim. Ethnic needs were dominant with little concern about citizen needs.

Negotiations with the tribe only got under way when the old Sheikh died and his son took his place. The son adopted a different approach. Being young and educated, he wished to move to a planned settlement where modern services were provided. He quickly reached an agreement with the Implementation Authority.[2]

The Planner describes the gap between the generations which was clearly evident in a meeting which he attended to discuss with them the move to Aruar:

> "We were sitting there and the young Bedouin said: 'If you want to satisfy us, build us a neighbourhood in this area'. I said we cannot build it there (because it was far from the actual settlement site) but we will build it in another area, and so on. It was my job to represent the perspective of the planner rather than the Bedouin, so the negotiation continued and I felt that it was a waste of time. Tea and cookies and more tea, and how are you and how do you feel, they were so nice, but stubborn, and I was stubborn as well, and when we finished and went out, the young Bedouin said: 'Look, the old man (his father, the Sheikh) is very sick.' — the old man was there all the time — 'He is very sick and he is going to die.' I didn't understand the message and took it as a medical report about the old man's condition. Only afterwards did the chief negotiator explain to me the hidden meaning: 'They are saying they cannot accept your offer as long as the old man is alive because they respect him and know he will not accept it. But as soon as the old man is dead they can negotiate.' In fact it went exactly as they suggested, the old man died and soon afterwards the young Bedouin came to negotiate and later on they rushed me with the planning and implementation."

This event, which repeated itself several times in the cases of other tribes, illustrated the different leanings of the older and younger Bedouin, and different balance of ethnic and citizen needs. For the younger generation, citizen needs were uppermost. They wished to move into a planned settlement with infrastructure and services, unlike their parents who wanted to hold on to their ethnic identity through landownership and were reluctant to leave their land. Infrastructure and services was not important enough a reason to give up the tribe's heritage.

Besides the dominance of the younger generation there was another reason why the Abu Gweid were more ready to move to a planned settlement than the Abu Rebeha. Their ethnic needs were different. They did not need to maintain the position of the leading tribe in Bedouin society as did the Abu Rebeha, and although they also considered landownership important, it was not a tool to preserve their status as it was for the Abu Rebeha.

Conclusions

The analysis of the participation of the Abu Arar, Abu Rebeha and Abu Gweid represents three examples of how differences in class and age groups had a tremendous influence on the responses of each of the groups towards state plans because of the different balance of their ethnic and citizen needs. The negotiations with the Abu Arar Fellahin and the younger generation of Abu Gweid shows that when their citizen needs took precedence over their ethnic needs, they gained a certain degree of empowerment, and pluralist needs were more easily met at the planning level.

In contrast, the Abu Rebeha tribe's pluralist needs leaned more toward their ethnic identity which was not acknowledged by the State, despite drastic changes of the Kessifa plan to meet their initial demands. Where agreements were reached, the gulf between ethnic and citizen needs was bridged.

Understanding the ethnic complexities of the different Bedouin tribes and Fellahin groups facilitated the process of providing them with appropriate living solutions which answer their citizen needs.

3.5. PARTICIPATION AS A TOOL FOR ADDRESSING ETHNIC AND CITIZEN NEEDS

The participation of ethnic groups in development projects is a crucial component in addressing ethnic and citizen needs in settlement planning. This is a new dimension of the debate around participation about which not enough has been written. The role of participation both as an institutional and management issue in the settlement planning process is the focus of this chapter. It highlights the influence of the heterogeneity of beneficiaries as well as policy makers and planners on the nature of participation and its outcomes. The case study of the participation of the Bedouin in the evacuation and resettlement project constitutes the major example in analysing this complicated and rather new issue. The participation of the Bedouin is analysed through the three stages of the project and this in depth analysis provides the tools for creating general guidelines for participation of ethnic groups in a development process. The discussion on participation in this section centres on the conceptual analysis of the debate and relates to four main issues: why participation, whose participation, how participation, when participation and participation in what?

3.5.1. Why participation?

Answering the question of 'Why participation?' in this project provides an interesting illustration of how complex it is to analyse the meaning of participation. Participation was introduced by a body called the Bedouin Team,[3] in fact, for two almost opposite reasons. It was the Bedouin's right as citizens to be involved in solutions determining their life situations. But participation was also employed in order to reduce Bedouin objections to government plans connected with the Landownership Law and the planned settlements.

The inclusion of participation to meet the Bedouin's rights can be seen as part of the pluralist orientation of the Bedouin Team. This is illustrated in the chief negotiator's views. Living in a Kibbutz where one of the basic principles is the participation of its members in decision-making, he made it clear from the outset that participation must be included in the Team's policies:

> "I had a clear view on this issue. It could not be that I live in a Kibbutz where plans that are made for me take into consideration what I want (and for the Bedouin not) so I thought we had to do the same for the Bedouin. It is true that the Bedouin's understanding in planning is minor, but my understanding in planning at the beginning was minor as well. Through mutual work the planner convinces the citizen."

The chief negotiator suggested the use of participation to achieve greater equality and also to identify the needs of the Bedouin. His involvement in Bedouin matters was rather personal — that of someone who lived in the area and was concerned about the future relationships between Bedouin and Jews.

Participation was perceived as the citizen's right to influence decisions concerning the life of an individual,

> "For the first time it was agreed that there is a need to negotiate with the Bedouin themselves and that the Bedouin have the right to present their case. This was the first principle of the Bedouin Team, to negotiate with the Bedouin."
>
> (Marx, 1982, p. 39)

At this stage in the project, participation was adopted in order to achieve greater equality for the Bedouin as a segment within Israeli society in accordance with:

> "people's right and duty to participate in the execution (i.e. planning, implementation and management) of projects which profoundly affect their life."
>
> (UN, Habitat, 1984, p. 6)

This was alluded to in what the chief negotiator said in response to a conference of representatives of Jewish Settlers in the Negev:

> "The Bedouin are citizens of the Negev. As a result of our ignorance of their existence they were deprived to the extent that in the present situation 42,000 citizens are considered second class citizens. We must consider them as equal neighbours and involve them in the development process. The Bedouin are equal citizens of the Negev and it is their right to live in the Negev in dignity and to settle in planned settlements. Only close cooperation will bring harmony and a mutual understanding between settlers in the Negev."

It should be noted that, even when talking about participation in the context of citizen rights, it was not meant that participation should lead to true Bedouin empowerment, but more that it should become a way to convince them that government plans were truly suitable for them. During the project, especially when the Implementation Authority started negotiating with each Bedouin clan, the Authority was really only paying lip service to the idea of participation. In fact, it was simply used as a means to reduce Bedouin objections to the government's intention to evacuate them from Tel Malhata. The Implementation Authority thought that Bedouin agreement to government policy would be achieved by their participation in the identification of their needs when formulating revised plans involving the Landownership Law and the planned Bedouin settlements. The government for its part had seen that evacuating them by force was not an appropriate solution, and thus the only other option available was the participation of the Bedouin in the planning process (Ben Meir, 14.7.1988). These two different reasons for encouraging participation were expressed in the following quotes from members of the Bedouin Team:

> "I would not say full participation in decision-making, but I believe in a compromise between forcing someone and letting him participate (in the decision making process). There is no clear cut way of doing it. It was a logical outcome not a goal in itself."

> "The only way to prevent the violent objection of the Bedouin to any development plans in the area is by enabling their participation in the determination of their future. The participation of the Bedouin would create a clear distinction between practical daily problems and political national problems. This distinction is necessary for formulating an efficient solution to practical daily problems."

The planner was convinced that making this distinction between the two sets of problems and recognising their equal importance would encourage the Bedouin to cooperate. Reduction of Bedouin objections would ensure the peaceful implementation of government plans to build the new airfield:

> "We knew that we must do something otherwise there would not be an airfield, so we initiated meetings with the Bedouin through that man (who later became the chief negotiator). He passed the message to the Bedouin. On the Bedouin side it was the Sheikh Hamad Abu Rebeha who organized the Bedouin."

Besides being involved in the re-formulation of the Landownership Law, the Bedouin also participated in the settlement planning process at its various levels. But during the early stages of negotiation the only issue that the Bedouin Team discussed with the Bedouin was the internal layout of the planned settlements (meeting with Bedouin, Agenda of 25.10.1979). The Bedouin however thought that the landownership conflict should be the main issue of the negotiation. As the planner mentioned:

> "We talked about the type of settlement desired. This was the main issue for us, but they (the Bedouin) told us: 'First let's talk about land arrangements.'"

Officially speaking, participation in the settlement planning process was introduced to better match the plans with Bedouin needs. As the head of the Implementation Authority noted:

> "The area in which participation is included as a declared policy is in the physical settlement planning. Besides that, any participation included was not based on an underlying policy."

In fact, their participation went beyond this, and continued to be significant as their needs were met when the level of planning became more detailed.

The different approaches to the inclusion of participation illustrates the heterogeneous nature of the Bedouin Team itself, resulting from different personal views that each of its members held towards the role of participation, such as the chief negotiator on the one hand and the Head of the Implementation Authority on the other. This influenced the whole process of negotiation with the Bedouin throughout its different stages as further analysed.

3.5.2. Whose participation? and how participation?

In the early stages of the project, only the important sheikhs negotiated with government representatives. The participants were the leaders of the leading tribes in the Negev, including those of the evacuated tribes. The Bedouin Team accepted official custom by which sheikhs represented the tribes, although in reality there were several separate interest groups within the tribes. Participation at this stage was not community participation but rather, as defined by Hollesteiner (1977), that of the local élite, where a community is represented by its leaders, leaving the majority of the community out of the process. The chief negotiator described the way in which participation of the elite was conducted:

> "I formulated a committee of seven sheikhs from the Tel Malhata area and I told each of them to bring representatives from two clans. Besides this forum, there was a committee of all the sheikhs in the Negev. I used to invite them, talk to them about general issues and then I would meet only the sheikhs from Tel Malhata. It started as a sporadic action but became a tradition."

It was participation of only an élite group but since such an élite was the traditional mouthpiece of Bedouin society it was compatible with their ethnic needs at least in the early stages of the project. At this first stage the Bedouin appeared to be a strongly united homogeneous group whose position in negotiation was strong because they had a common interest: to reach as satisfactory a land agreement as possible. The land issues concerned not only those who had been evacuated, but all the Bedouin of the Negev.

The Bedouin's main representative was a dominant figure: Sheikh Hamad Abu Rebeha. Being the only Bedouin Member of the Knesset (the Israeli Parlaiment) he was the obvious choice to be their main spokesman. Regrettably for the Bedouin, he was assassinated in 1981 because of unrelated political rivalry with the Druze. His assassination caused a temporary halt in the negotiation process, as he was one of the major mediators between the Israeli authorities and the Bedouin.

One of the consequences of this event was that the united front of the Bedouin vanished. The participation was extended from the inclusion of only seven sheikhs to the inclusion of each tribe's leaders. When detailed negotiations started, the separate needs of the different sub-groups affected the unity of the Bedouin and weakened their powerful position in the negotiation process. As we have seen in the previous section, the Fellahin, who were the first to negotiate, benefited most from this process, and their newly powerful position in the negotiations led to their obtaining their demands.

Perhaps more interesting was the increasing participation of the younger generation and their greater influence in Bedouin society as a result of this new involvement. The participatory factor in this project served to accelerate a process leading to the growing dominance of the younger generation of Bedouin and changed the relationship between them and the older generation (Ben Meir, 14.7.1988). The two issues of class and age within Bedouin society and the different needs of the respective groups provided an opening for the authorities to break the apparent homogeneity of the Bedouin and to gain position in negotiations as seen in the previous section.

Participation of Bedouin through the different stages of the project can be identified as consultation and even decision-making. This was particularly so at the first stage when the revision of the Landownership Law was the major issue. The Bedouin leaders were then consulted on different alternatives suggested by the Bedouin Team to the various issues at stake in the law. At this level, the participation of only the élite group was allowed on this main issue as the chief negotiator mentioned:

> "Participation started from the first stage, the re-formulation of the law. We knew that we had to reach an agreement and compromise with the Bedouin in the revised law. The government bureaucrats wanted to show that they are good (i.e. demonstrate their loyalty to their superiors) by giving the Bedouin less compensation, and we had to fight for it. We offered more and negotiated with the government officials up to the point that we felt that the Bedouin had to compromise. For example, the (question of the) size of irrigated land. It was previously 1% of their land. The Bedouin wanted 7% and we compromised on 5% of their land with irrigation."

The sole participation of only the élite groups changed during the negotiation process as the discussion went deeper. At the first stage, discussions involving only élite groups included changes in the Landownership Law relating to issues such as the size of plots and the size of irrigated land, and the determination of the number and type of settlements. During the evacuation of the Bedouin from the airfield site, their leaders were consulted over the proposed timetable for the move. The actual evacuation was delayed several times because of the harvest season and for other reasons. On these occasions the chief negotiator played the role of mediator between the army, with its strict demand for a quick removal, and the Bedouin.

In fact, instead of a period of three months for evacuation as specified by the new Landownership Law, the process took three years, mainly because of the slowness of the process of negotiation with the Bedouin. This of course gave rise to much criticism from the government, who questioned the necessity for delaying the project because of Bedouin demands.

At the second stage, leaders of clans (Hamulas) also participated in determining the site location of the planned settlements and the location of neighbourhoods within the settlements. During the later stages, heads of households and extended families participated in planning the inner structure of their neighbourhoods and the allocation of their plots. As the planning process became more detailed their participation took the form of decision-making. At this stage their demands were more influential in changing the proposed plans. But in fact, the more detailed the plans became and the more the Bedouin participated in the planning process, the more difficult to implement it became. The plans which were changed according to the Bedouin's suggestions led to the creation of very inefficient schemes which were difficult to implement.

A participatory factor was included in this project from its inception, starting with the plan's formulation and continuing through the whole project cycle through ongoing consultations (Hollestiener, 1977). But it changed in nature and effect as the project developed, from a promising desire to indulge the exercising of citizen rights, to a mere technical tool to reduce the force of Bedouin objections. These changes in the nature and power of participation were affected by the differing personal approaches to the issue of participation held by each member of the Team. There then followed the organisational shift of the arbitrating body, from Bedouin Team to Implementation Authority, i.e. from a pressure advocate group to a bureaucratic executive.

3.5.3. When participation?

As noted in Chapter 2, most experience shows that participation which is included at the decision-making level is a precondition if the objective is empowerment, whereas where participation is a means to achieve a development objective it is usually employed only at the implementation and maintenance level (Moser, 1989b). Participation in this project was an interesting phenomenon because of its inclusion at the decision-making level, and in fact at all stages of the project, because it did not ensure empowerment for all the Bedouin en masse, but rather only for certain groups like the Fellahin and the younger generation.

The question of whether the advocacy strategy of the Bedouin Team and the participation of the Bedouin in the planning process indeed led to a greater meeting of their pluralist needs is now investigated in two issues: the revised version of the Landownership Law, and the number and type of planned Bedouin settlements.

3.5.4. *Participation in what?*

Participation took place in principle matters which determined the whole process of evacuation and re-settlement: the revision of Landownership Law and the number and type of planned Bedouin settlements.

The revision of the Landownership Law

The main task of the Bedouin Team was to revise the landownership proposals of 1979 which were firmly rejected by Bedouin and Jews alike. The Bedouin Team formulated the principles for a revised Landownership Law listed and explained below.

(a) Determining Bedouin rights to compensation.

The re-formulation of the Landownership Law represented a different approach to Bedouin legal rights concerning their land claims. The 1979 version upheld the official policy by which the state only partially recognised these rights, and the periods of landholding and of cultivating the land uninterruptedly determined the level of compensation. The longer the Bedouin held and cultivated the land, the higher the percentage of its value they would receive. Moreover, the value of land was still determined only according to its market value in 1948 before any development took place in the Negev, which, as we have seen was much lower than the current true value.

The Bedouin strongly objected to this principle and claimed that they would never leave their land if these were the compensations they got. The Bedouin Team realised that this was the main obstacle in the law and therefore the revised law was much more generous in determining their rights and the level of compensation they ought to get.

In contrast, the revised version of the law emphasised Bedouin rights to full compensation for lands they lived on and had cultivated prior to two dates (either 1.1.1979 or 8.7.1980, depending on the particular area). The Bedouin were also paid the realistic market value for their land, 2.5–3.5 times more than was offered to them by the 1979 version. This approach treated all landholders equally and now perceived them as owners of land, avoiding the former requirement to prove landownership and cultivation. In this respect the revised version was undoubtedly an improvement of the original law.

(b) The exchange principle.

The exchange principle is another component which determined a more egalitarian approach to negotiation with the Bedouin. The exchange principle was based on the Bedouin Team determination that compensation should be based on the idea of commercial transactions undertaken on an exchange basis. This principle recognised for the first time, Bedouin owned assets for which they were entitled to full remuneration. Each of the properties involved was to be financially assessed at its market value: the land and property the Bedouin surrendered to the State and what the State would provide to the Bedouin in return, i.e. irrigated plots, domestic plots, etc. The Bedouin got compensation according to the size of the land they handed to the state and the value of other property they had, and this was to be assessed by an independent assessor. Similarly, whatever property the Bedouin received from the State was also financially valued. The two sets of properties were to be set off one against the other. If the balance showed that the Bedouin owed money to the State, which was normally the case for former non-landowners like the Fellahin who wanted to acquire more than one dunam, then they would be treated like any other citizen and have to pay for their land.

The Bedouin would get, in return for their land, developed plots supported by a full infrastructure of water supply, roads and electricity in one of the two settlements offered to them. The size of the plots varied from 1–3 dunam. Non-landowners and Bedouin who had up to 10 dunam were entitled to one dunam. To Bedouin who had 10–100 dunam, a plot of 2 dunam was offered, and those with 100 dunam and more got plots of 3 dunam. The first dunam of land was free, but for anything more the Bedouin was to pay the full market value. These were better conditions than the 1979 version of the law according to which Bedouin who gave up their land had the right to a plot in one of the six planned settlements proposed, one dunam to each Bedouin. The earlier they handed over their land, the less they had to pay for the new plot. Bedouin who handed over their land within ten weeks from the date mentioned in the law would get their plot free of charge.

The new 1980 version revised by the Bedouin Team improved the Bedouin's position by giving them larger irrigated plots for agriculture with greater supply of water.

Because the loss of land would deprive the Bedouin of their old economic base, they needed to be assured of a secure alternative livelihood. Therefore, they were also given the choice to receive financial compensation for their properties if they did not want to live in planned settlements. With the money, they could buy shops or taxis, for instance, or plots of land in other places not confined to the settlements. Indeed, some of the evacuated Bedouin used their compensation to move to villages outside the Negev area.

The size of the land expropriated was also reduced in the 1980 version of the law following a strong request of Bedouin which was supported by the Labour Party and the left wing parties. While 300,000 dunam (30,000 ha) of land was to be expropriated in the 1979 version of the law for building the airfield and the planned settlements, the Bedouin Team considered 80,000 dunam to be sufficient for all military and civil purposes. This calculation was based on the underlying

principle that the area expropriated for the airfield should be minimal so that
the Bedouin would not suspect that the government was taking advantage of the
situation in order to expropriate larger areas than were really needed for their
purposes. By suggesting a reduction in the size of land to be expropriated, the
Bedouin Team thought that they could minimise the Bedouin's objections.

(c) The first duman for free — different needs for different classes.

The debate around the provision of the first dunam for free illustrates how
different needs of different classes determine the processes and outcomes of
negotiation with the Bedouin. A first dunam for free was suggested in the 1979
version of the Landownership Law. The original idea of the first dunam for free
was inspired by the Labour Party, whose support was necessary for the law to be
revised. The Labour Party's principles, based on its socialist credo of equality,
demanded a first dunam for free in order to benefit the non-landowners, most of
whom were living in very poor conditions. But this principle was not in line with
the traditions of Bedouin society, because it worked against the landowners who
still felt that they were entitled to more than non-landowners. But, because of
pressure from the Labour Party, the first dunam for free was included in the new
1980 version of the law in spite of the Bedouin Team's objections.

The Bedouin Team originally objected to this idea because it contradicted
the exchange principle. They argued that no 'gifts' should be provided by the
State, but that all commodities be financially valued. This principle was in line
with the desire to treat the Bedouin as equal citizens in the new 'fair exchange'
arrangement. In deciding upon the exchange principle and abandoning the
idea of a free dunam, the reliance of the Bedouin on State subsidies would be
reduced. The Bedouin Team feared that providing a free plot would perpetuate
the dependency of the Bedouin on the bureaucracy, a situation which tended
to recur in Israel whenever easy incentives or 'gifts' were on offer. Therefore,
no gifts would be provided to them, but they would get the message that both
their land and property and the building plots in the new settlements were
valuable commodities. All transactions would take the form of negotiated deals
(Marx, 1988).

This was a different approach to the paternalistic tone of the 1979 law by which
the Bedouin got less money because their land rights were still not recognised,
but at the same time they were provided with the 'gift' of the one dunam free to
help them in their poor conditions. This system which supported poor groups by
subsidies created continuous dependency. It also, as we have seen, characterised
state policies towards the residents of the development towns. In order to narrow
social and economic gaps, the state supported the residents with a subsidising
system, but this only caused further dependency on subsidies, rather than
encouraging the recipients to become responsible for their own lives. The residents
of the Jewish development towns, for instance, had fallen into this trap with the

Neighbourhood Renewal Project and become over-reliant on bureaucratic systems when provided with new services (Shahak, 10.8.1988).

Another argument against the principle of the first dunam for free was that its provision constituted discrimination against landowners as opposed to non-landowners. This discrimination was further aggravated by the fact that 'real' Bedouin landowners lived off their lands and were not integrated into the modern job market like the Fellahin, most of whom already had been given plots of land in planned settlements. This argument was stated by another member of the Bedouin Team:

> "that is why the first dunam for free is a distortion. Because the group we are interested in are the landowners. As one Bedouin has said: Justice is not equality and equality is not Justice and the Bedouin want justice. The Bedouin claim that the Jews and the Labour Party are too egalitarian for them and the first dunam free reflects an equality approach, not justice. We (the Bedouin Team) said we want justice and I supported this approach. If you (Bedouin) have more land you get more money and vice versa you get government support but not a dunam for free as a gift only because you are Bedouin. The Labour Party objected to this principle because it is an egalitarian party."

The debate about the first dunam for free highlights the fact that there is not any one set of Bedouins needs, but different sets of needs that vary according to the different classes in Bedouin society. For landowners a first dunam for free went against their ethnic need to maintain their status above non-landowners, while the latter's ethnic needs to become independent of the 'real Bedouin' were met.

This example illustrates the importance of identifying the level of heterogeneity or homogeneity of the different sub-groups within Bedouin society. The assumption that a society has only one set of interests can clearly be challenged here. The issue of homogeneity and heterogeneity in society has been raised by several scholars. Moser (1989) points out the tendency to assume that 'the community' is homogeneous without clarification, whether it refers to a spatial or social grouping. Molyneux (1985) refers to the assumptions of homogeneity in the fight for women's interests. She mentions the importance of the recognition of differences rather than similarity in any study of women's capacity to struggle and benefit from social change.

Many examples could be brought to emphasise the major effects of heterogeneity of a society on participation processes and its outcomes. One such example is farmer's participation in an irrigation project in Bhairawa-Lumbini in Nepal.[4] In this project the participation of farmers is mainly aimed at taking over the operation and maintenance of the deep tubewells system which was built in the area with the financial support of the World Bank. Another component of participation is the cost sharing — the farmers were asked to pay water charges. The whole process of taking over is expected to be carried out through water users associations—special bodies created in the project area. The farmers continuously

expressed their reluctancy to take over. The official explanation is that their refusal arose mainly because of their reluctancy to pay water charges. But recent field survey revealed that the necessity to pay is not the main reason for farmers reluctancy to take over but the fact that farmers do not cooperate through the water users associations, as these institutions do not operate at all, and therefore the farmers are anxious not to take on such responsibilities themselves. One of the assumptions yet to be investigated for the poor functioning of the water users associations is the ethnic heterogeneity of their members and the social and traditional constraints to cooperate in one organisational unit. This arises from the different needs and interests of each ethnic group which lives in the area (many immigrants from all over Nepal and neighbouring India in which many castes and untouchable groups exist). Cooperation between these groups hardly exists.

In Bedouin society, heterogeneity was such that almost every sub-group had its own set of needs. These needs sometimes clashed with the needs of other sub-groups, as with the clashes between landowners and non-landowners, with the former basing their existence on agriculture and the latter being more integrated into the Israeli economy. The different needs of old and younger generations are another example of the heterogeneous character of Bedouin society. The young are geared towards modernisation while the old still seek to maintain the traditional lifestyle. These differences in needs clearly influence the nature of participation and its outcomes and must be taken into consideration when formulating plans to meet ethnic groups needs and when basing development projects on participation of beneficiaries.

The number and type of settlements for the evacuated Bedouin — an emphasis for discrimination

The conflict between the Bedouin and the State over the issue of the number and type of planned settlements (see previous chapter) made for difficult negotiations between the Bedouin Team and the Bedouin. Two contrasting attitudes existed. The Bedouin, on the one hand, wished to build planned settlements for almost every individual clan, which in practice virtually meant the legalisation of their spontaneous settlements. The state, on the other, adapted the Master Plan's decisions suggesting the building of seven settlements for all the Bedouin in the Negev, and in a subsequently revised plan proposed six settlements solely for the evacuees from Tel Malhata.

The Bedouin Team in fact objected to both possibilities and took a much more radical stand, suggesting only two urban settlements in the new version of the Landownership Law. Its arguments favouring this option were similar to the official government policy: they reasoned that it was better to concentrate financial resources in two settlements so that the level of infrastructure, services and diversified employment opportunities would be higher. They feared that distributing the limited available resources into seven urban settlements would not result in the creation of satisfactory services (Marx, 1981). Bearing in mind the past experience of inadequate services in the development towns, the Bedouin Team were convinced that a large sized settlement would be the only feasible option for the reasonable provision of such services, with a minimum threshold of 15,000 inhabitants most desirable — a figure determined by the Israeli official planning standards authority.

> "The Bedouin who are moved to planned towns should get the same services and infrastructure as exist in Jewish settlements. It is not recommended that two standards be created, one for the Bedouin and one for the Jews. The Bedouin settlements should provide services which are needed by the Bedouin like primary schools, high schools, shops, commercial services, etc."
>
> (Marx, 1981, p. 235)

The need to provide facilities which would create diversified employment was the second reason for favouring large urban settlements:

> "We argue that urban-oriented settlements must be large, in contrast to rural settlements. In rural settlements all people are employed in one type of work and there is no need for diversification in services. The people would get outside services whereas in a town there is a diversification of employment."
>
> (Ibid)

The Bedouin Team's approach to diversified employment opportunities for the Bedouin was also expressed in the way that suggested compensation be channelled. As one of the Bedouin Team members expressed it:

> "within the process of (reaching) landownership solutions there is a necessity to find a means by which to channel the compensation paid to landowners to create alternative employment opportunities, mainly in industry near the planned settlements."

Initially, the Team intended to include these principles within the new law. But due to bureaucratic delaying tactics they were not included and only accepted later as unofficial agreements.

An alternative solution

Bedouin preferences still called for a different approach to finding the appropriate settlement solution, which would meet both ethnic and citizen needs. First, why not provide the Bedouin with the opportunity to choose their own way of life in various types of settlements, with the same freedom of choice available to the Jewish population, and each type of settlement meeting the different requirements of the different social groups? The Fellahin, for whom citizen needs took precedence over ethnic needs, would find an urban settlement more suitable, whereas for the 'real' Bedouin an agricultural settlement would be more appropriate. As one of the Bedouin expressed it:

"There is a necessity to offer alternatives. The authorities must offer alternatives. What
they offer now is only one alternative, to move to planned settlements of one type.
They do not offer other alternatives."

The lack of choice in this matter can again be identified as discrimination, with
different treatment given in handling people in a *similar* situation. The Bedouin,
although officially perceived as equal citizens, did not have the opportunity to
freely choose which type of settlement they were to live in.

In this regard, the Bedouin Team investigated the option of building a
rural settlement on the lines of the Israeli Moshav (a small, loosely structured
cooperative). Many Bedouin wished to live in such a settlement, but once they
realised that Moshav lands were not privately owned but state land, they rejected
the idea. But the question still remained why there was no specific settlement
model which would meet the Bedouin's pluralist needs — a settlement based
on the pattern of the Israeli Moshav but also recognising Bedouin needs of
landownership. Such an idea was suggested by the Association for Civil Rights
in Israel. It suggested providing the Bedouin with several types of settlements:
urban or semi-urban, agricultural and based on irrigated lands, agricultural and
based on animal raising, and a settlement with a combination of the last two (a
proposal for land arrangements, 2.4.1979). These options would be offered to
all Bedouin in the Negev with preference given to those evacuated from the Tel
Malhata area. Each rural settlement would be constructed for only 100 families
each. They would be built on land owned by the residents. The agricultural land
would be leased as in the Jewish rural sector. The services for these different
settlements would be provided in a central location. This combination would
satisfy both ethnic and citizen needs. Moreover, calculations of the financial cost
of such settlements suggested that they would not be as expensive as previously
feared. The Association did not include the expenditure on infrastructure because
they argued this could be developed independently in any type of settlement (the
Association for Civil Rights in Israel, 2.4.1979).

But this possibility was rejected by the Bedouin Team, who still maintained
that the Bedouin would be better off in urban settlements, especially in terms
of the infrastructure provided, but also because they feared that these proposals
would create an unmanageable precedent, with the Bedouin demanding a separate
settlement for each clan, and with their spatial dispersion remaining the same as
that of the spontaneous settlements.

Eventually, the need for freedom to choose where to live was partly addressed
by the provision in the law that the Bedouin could get financial compensation and
invest wherever they wished, and not necessarily in the planned settlements — a
choice which some of the sub-groups took.

To conclude, it is clear that the two major issues — landownership and the
type and number of planned settlements — were not resolved in the process of
planning in this project in spite of Bedouin participation in the planning process.

But, because of the different power relations for different groups within the negotiation process, some groups in fact had gradually succeeded in obtaining a certain degree of response to their demands. But for the majority of Bedouin the proposals only went a short way to meeting their pluralist needs. It can therefore be concluded that participation in this case had not promoted meeting Bedouin pluralist needs.

Another conclusion that can be drawn from this chapter is that the more heterogeneous a society is, the more complicated it is to address the needs of each of the sub-groups. In the example of the Bedouin, the power of each of the groups in the negotiation process played a major role in addressing the groups needs and in making their participation more meaningful.

NOTES: CHAPTER 3

1. In a situation of ethnic minorities struggle for political separation, as the case of the Soviet Union, the whole approach of ethnic and citizen needs within a situation of pluralism is not relevant.

2. The Implementation Authority is the regulative body created according to the 1980 Landownership Law to negotiate with the Bedouin on matters of compensations and the evacuation to the planned settlements. The Implementation Authority consisted of a Negotiation Team, Planning Team, Finance and Accounting section and Think Tank. The Think Tank consisted of former Bedouin Team members.

3. The Bedouin Team was the first team to negotiate with the Bedouin. It consisted of non-governmental professionals who were members of the Negev Team, a team created by the Ministry of Interior to re-plan the Negev region as a response to the Israeli Defense Forces withdrawal from Sinai as determined by the Peace Treaty with Egypt. The Bedouin Team initiated the first negotiations with the Bedouin with a more open view regarding issues at stake as a result of the necessity to evacuate them from Tel Malhata. Government officials held different ideas less advanced in nature on these matters. Some of these differences between the two approaches will be presented in the chapter.

4. This project is planned by Tahal Consulting Engineers — Israel and financed by the World Bank. The data is based on a socio-economic survey held in the area in November 1991.

CHAPTER 4

Conclusions

The major conclusion issuing from the study is that the pluralist needs must be taken into consideration in planning and implementing development schemes for ethnic groups, particularly those in transition or social change. In such schemes, a framework of the two kinds of needs, their combination in a concept of pluralist needs, and a definition of discrimination in this context must be fundamental ingredients. This approach would greatly ease the process of social change, while maintaining social, political and economic stability within the society as a whole. From analysis of the case study, practical conclusions can be drawn which perhaps could become guidelines for policy-makers and planners working towards a situation of cultural pluralism, making room for the participation of beneficiaries in the plan-making process.

A planning process in cultural pluralism is suggested to include the following stages:

(1) Identification of pluralist needs. The first task seems to be the identification of ethnic minority pluralist needs. This is a slow process necessitating the constant attention of anthropologists and social workers. Many techniques can be used at this stage: historical and ethnographical documents, interviews, questionnaires and observations, all of them aimed at finding out what is the social, economic and political structure of the society, and what are the pluralist needs of each of its constituent groups.

This step should be carried out with the participation of beneficiaries in identifying the heterogeneity of groups, their separate needs and the contradictions in their needs that might occur.

The results of this investigation should help in the creation of a framework for one or several sets of pluralist needs of the society. This is a crucial and fundamental stage in the process of pluralist planning, since societies are not homogeneous as has been seen in the case of the Bedouin. Each sub-group has its own sets of needs. Needs are also dynamic factors and change with time, and this must also be taken into consideration.

(2) The plan-making process. Groups of architects, social planners and economists should work on the translation of pluralist needs into several alternative plans and should make cost estimates for each of the alternatives,

ascertaining their financial, social and political applicability and investigating practical ways of implementing each of them. Only alternatives which are suitable according to these components should be introduced to the beneficiaries.

(3) Discussion with the beneficiaries on the alternatives suggested. This stage should be carried out with social or community workers to facilitate the translation of plans to the beneficiaries lacking technical knowledge or speaking a different language. This should relate to every level of planning. For example, if the target is a settlement, discussions should focus on the structure of the settlement itself and the nature of neighbourhoods, down to the type of houses built. At the end of this process, the desired alternative must be selected. Issues such as: participation who, how participation, when participation should be determined at the outset, aiming at involving as many beneficiaries as possible at different levels of planning. Special techniques should be adopted to make alternative plans clear and understandable to the beneficiaries and to ensure that all planning components are known to beneficiaries.

(4) The implementation stage. The implementation of the chosen plan should be carried out by a team which includes representatives of the beneficiaries, government officials, anthropologists, social planners and community workers. Besides the physical implementation of the plans, the community workers should guide and assist the beneficiaries in the process of implementation of their plan and the actual evacuation to the settlement. Patient community assistance would create and foster a local leadership which would later take charge of the settlement. A deliberately slow process would allow the beneficiaries to adapt to the changes they will face and the new way of life they will be exposed to. This is an example of a plan-making process for a settlement, but it could also be implemented in any other area where policies or plans are made for ethnic groups in transition. For example, special curriculums could be designed for ethnic groups combining their traditional education with a more advanced education system. Equally traditional and modern health methods could be combined.

The story of the relationships between the majority–minority ethnic groups as seen through the prism of ethnicity in this monograph and the pluralism desired in the settlement planning process of Israeli development schemes for the Negev Bedouin, contributes, it is hoped, to the formulation of an operational framework combining within it the issues of pluralism, needs and participation. The use of the operational framework created in the monograph can be viewed as an attempt to translate cultural differences into planning schemes, and the four guidelines, it is hoped, can give direction to policy-makers and planners faced with the conflicts of ethnicity and citizenship, so that a more viable environment can be achieved to bring stability to diversified societies such as Israel's. It is undoubtedly a complicated and controversial process but it might be the only option left to divided societies living in one political unit.

Bibliography

Books and Articles

ABU REBEHA, H. (1982) Land uses among the Bedouins, *Notes on the Bedouin*, **13**, 3–8 (in Hebrew).

ABU REBEHA, Y. (1979) The Bedouins' aspirations, *Notes on the Bedouin*, **10**, 31–36 (in Hebrew).

ABU-JABER, K. S. and GHARAIBEH, A. (1980) Bedouin settlement: organizational, legal and administrative structure — the experience of Jordan, University of Jordan, Aman, Mimeo.

AKZIN, B. and DROR, Y. (1966) *Israel: High pressure planning*, Syracuse University Press, New York.

AMIRAN, D., SHINAR, A. and BEN DAVID, Y. (1979) The Bedouin settlements in the Be'er Sheva Valley, In: A. Shmueli and Y. Gradus (eds), *The Land of the Negev*, pp. 652–665. The Ministry of Defense Publications, Tel Aviv (in Hebrew).

AMIT, D. (1982) Legal problems concerning the Bedouin situation in the state of Israel, *Notes on the Bedouins*, **10**, 11–21 (in Hebrew).

ARENSTEIN, S. R. (1969) Ladder of citizen participation, *Journal of the American Institute of Planners*, **35**, 216–224.

BEN DAVID, J. (1976) The process of spontaneous settlements among the Negev Bedouin, In: C. Bailey (ed.), *Notes on the Bedouin*, **7**, 30–49 (in Hebrew).

BEN DAVID, J. (1982) Stages in the sedentarization of the Negev Bedouin: a transition from former semi-nomadic to settled population, Thesis submitted for the degree of Doctor of Philosophy, Jerusalem (in Hebrew).

BEN DAVID, J. (1988) *Agricultural Settlements for the Bedouin Population — Policy Proposal*, The Jerusalem Institute for Research, Jerusalem (in Hebrew).

BRUTZKUS, E. (1964) *Physical Planning in Israel*, Department of Interior, Jerusalem.

CENTRAL BEAUREAU OF STATISTICS (1982) *Statistical Abstract of Israel, Jerusalem*, No. 32.

CENTRAL BEAUREAU OF STATISTICS (1989) *Statistical Abstract of Israel, Jerusalem*, No. 40.

CHANERY, H., AHLUWALLA, M., BELL, C., DULOY, J. and JOLLY, R. (1974) *Redistribution with Growth*, Oxford University Press, Oxford.

CONYERS, D. (1982) *An Introduction to Social Planning in the Third World*, John Wiley and Sons, Chichester.

CONYERS, D. (1985) Rural regional planning: towards an operational theory, *Progress in Planning*, **23**, 1–66.

DE KADT, E. (1982) Community participation for health: The case of Latin America, *World Development*, **10**(7).

DHAL, A. (1980) Pluralism revised, In: S. Ehrlich and G. I. Wootton (eds), *Three Faces in Pluralism*, Gower, London.

FENSTER, T. (1991) Participation in the settlement planning process — the case of the Bedouin in the Israeli Negev, Unpublished Ph.D Dissertation, London School of Economics, London.

FURNIVALL, J. S. (1939) *The Netherlands India: Colonial Policy and Practice*, Cambridge University Press, Cambridge.

GILBERT, A. and WARD, P. (1984) Community action by the urban poor: democratic involvement, community self help or a means of social control, *World Development*, **12**(8), 769–782.

GLAZER, N. (1982) *Ethnic Dilemmas 1964–1982*, Cambridge University Press, Cambridge.

GLAZER, N. and MOYNIHAN, D. (eds)(1975) *Ethnicity: Theory and Experience*, Cambridge University Press, Cambridge.

GOLANY, G. (ed.)(1979) *Arid Zones Settlement Planning, the Israeli Experience*, pp. 3–42. Pergamon Press, New York.

GOLDBERG, B. and GREER, C. (1990) American visions, ethnic dreams: Public ethnicity and the sociological imagination, *Race and Relations Abstracts*, **15**(1), 6–60.

GORDON, N. (1964) *Assimilation in American Life: The Role of Race, Religion and National Origins*, Oxford University Press, New York.

GORNI, Y. (1979) Four basic approaches to the Arab problem, In: Y. Pedan (ed.), *Dreams and Realizations — Philosophy and Practice in Zionism*, pp. 55–72. The Ministry of Defence Publications, Tel Aviv (in Hebrew).

HALL, A. (1986) Community participation and rural development, In: J. Midgley (ed.), *Community Participation, Social Development and the State*, pp. 87–104. Methuen, London.

HAVAKUK, Y. (1983) Beit Ash Sha'ar — the traditional Bedouins' dwelling, *Notes on the Bedouin*, **14**, 31–71 (in Hebrew).

HERTZBERG, A. (1970) *The Zionist Idea*, Keter Publications, Tel Aviv (in Hebrew).

HOLLESTEINER, M. R. (1977) Power People, *Assignment Children*, **40**, 11–47.

HOLLESTEINER, M. R. (1982) Government strategies in urban areas and community participation, *Assignment Children*, **57/58**, 43–64.

HONDET, G. (1979) Tel Sheva — a planned Bedouin settlement, In: A. Shmueli and Y. Gradus (eds), *The Land of the Negev*, pp. 666–672. The Ministry of Defense Publications, Tel Aviv (in Hebrew).

HORNER, D. F. (1982) Planning for the Bedouin: the case of Tel Sheva, *Third World Planning Review*, **4**, 159–176.

ILO (1976) *Employment, Growth and Basic Needs, A One World Problem*, ILO, Geneva.

JACQUE, J. P. (1985) The principle of equality in economic law, *Common Market Law Review*, **22**, 135–142.

JAKUBOWSKA, L. A. (1984) The Bedouin family in Rahat: perspectives on social change, *Notes on the Bedouin*, **15**, 1E–24E.

JOO, R. (1991) Slovenes in Hungary and Hungarians in Slovenia: ethnic and state identity, *Ethnic and Racial Studies*, **14**(1), 101–106.

KAPLAN, A. and AMIT, Y. (1979b) *Planning for the Bedouin*, Mimeo (in Hebrew).

KAPLAN, A., AMIT, Y., SHMUELLY, A., TREITEL, P. and MORE, U. (1979a) *Master Plan of Bedouin Settlement*, Mimeo (in Hebrew).

KLIOT, N. and MEDZINI, A. (1985) Bedouin settlement policy in Israel, 1964–1982: another perspective, *Geoforum*, **16**, 428–439.

KUPER, L. and SMITH, M. G. (1969) *Pluralism in Africa*, University of California Press, Los Angeles.

MARX, E. (1967) *Bedouin of the Negev*, Manchester University Press, Manchester.

MARX, E. (1973) The ecological structure of the Bedouin society, In: Y. Eini and E. Orion (eds), *The Bedouin*, pp. 73–95. Midreshet Sde Boker, Ben Gurion University in the Negev, Sde Boker (in Hebrew).

MARX, E. (1977) The tribe as a unit of subsistence — nomadic pastoralism in the Middle East, *American Anthropologist*, **79**, 343–363.

MARX, E. (1980) Economic changes among Bedouin in the last decade, *Notes on the Bedouin*, **11**, 3–11 (in Hebrew).

MARX, E. (1981) The evacuation of the Bedouin from Tel Malhata, In: Y. Eini and E. Orion (eds), *The Bedouin*, pp. 231–237. Midreshet Sde Boker, Ben Gurion University in the Negev (in Hebrew).

MARX, E. (1988) *Advocacy in a Bedouin Resettlement Project*, 12th International Congress of Anthropological and Ecological Science, Mimeo.

MARX, E. and SHELA, M. (1979) The situation of the Bedouin in the Negev, In: Tahal Consulting Engineers (1979), *A Proposal for Evaluation and Resettlement of the Bedouin of Tel Malhata*, Appendix 1. Tel Aviv (in Hebrew).

MAYO, M. (1975) Community development — a radical alternative, In: R. Bailey and M. Brake (eds), *Radical Social Work*, pp. 129–143. Arnold, London.

MIDGLEY, J. (1986) *Community Participation, Social Development and the State*, Methuen, London.

MOLYNEUX, M. (1985) Mobilization without emancipation? Women's interests, the state, and revolution in Nicaragua, *Feminist Studies*, **11**, 227–254.

MOSER, C. (1983) The problem of evaluating community participation in urban development projects, In: C. Moser (ed.), Evaluating Community Participation in Urban Development Projects, *Development Planning Unit Working Paper*, London, **14**, 3–6.

MOSER, C. (1989a) Gender planning in the Third World: Meeting practical and strategic gender needs, *World Development*, **17**(11), 1799–1825.

MOSER, C. (1989b) Community participation in urban development projects in the Third World, *Progress in Planning*, **32**, 71–133.

MOSER, C. and LEVY, C. (1986) A theory and methodology of gender planning: meeting womens' practical and strategic needs, *Gender and Planning Workshop Paper*, London, **11**.

OAKLEY, P. and MARSDEN, D. (1984) *Approaches to Participation in Rural Development*, ILO, Geneva.

PAUL, S. (1986) Community participation in development projects: The World Bank experience, *World Bank Discussion Papers*, 6.

PEARSE, A. and STIEFEL, M. (1980) *Inquiry into Participation*, UNIRSD, Geneva.

PRAZANSKA, A. (1991) Ethnic conflicts in the context of democratizing political system, *Theory and Society*, **20**, 581–602.

RABUSHKA, A. and SHEPSLE, K. L. (1972) *Politics in Plural Societies*, Charles and Merrill Publishing Company, Ohio.

RAPPOPORT, A. (1978) Nomadism as a man–environment system, *Environment and Behaviour*, **10**(2), 214–247.

SANDBROOK, R. (1982) *The Politics of Basic Needs*, Heinemann, London.

SHELEF, L. S. (1990) *A Tribe is a Tribe is a Tribe — On Changing Social Concepts and Emerging Human Rights*, Tel Aviv University, Tel Aviv (Mimeo).

SKINNER, R. (1983a) Community participation: its scope and organization, In: R. Skinner and M. Rodell (eds), *People, Poverty and Shelter*, pp. 125–150. Methuen, London.

SKINNER, R. (1983b) A Peruvian popular participation policy and experience in sites services: Villa El Salvador, Lima, In: C. Moser (ed.), Evaluating Community Participation in Urban Development Projects, *Development Planning Unit Working Paper*, London, **14**, 34–44.

SMITH, M. G. (1965) *The Plural Society in the British West Indies*, University of California, Berkeley and Los Angeles.

SMOOHA, S. (1978) *Israel: Pluralism and Conflict*, University of California Press, Los Angeles.

STERN, E. and GRADUS, Y. (1979) Socio-cultural consideration in planning towns for nomads, *Ekistics*, **46**, 224–230.

STEWART, F. (1985) *Planning to Meet Basic Needs*, Macmillan, London.

STREETON, P. *et al.* (1981) *First Things First: Meeting Basic Human Needs in Developing Countries*, Oxford University Press, Oxford.

TAHAL CONSULTING ENGINEERS (1979) *A Proposal for Evaluation and Resettlement of the Bedouin of Tel Malhata*, Appendix 1. Tel Aviv (in Hebrew).

TAHAL CONSULTING ENGINEERS (1980) *Development Plan for the Negev*, Report No. 2. Tel Aviv (in Hebrew).

TAHAL CONSULTING ENGINEERS (1982) *Field Survey and Data Collection on the Bedouin in Be'er Sheva Valley*, prepared for the Government of Israel, in preparation for the removal and resettlement of the Bedouin of Tel Malhata (in Hebrew).

TAHAL CONSULTING ENGINEERS (1984) *The Project of Removal and Resettlement of the Bedouin of Tel Malhata*, Implementation Authority, Tel Aviv (in Hebrew).

TSUR, J. (1976) *Zionism*, New Brunswick, New Jersey.

UNCHS (1984) *Community Participation in the Execution of Squatter Settlement Upgrading Projects*, UN Centre for Human Settlement, Kenya.

UNITED NATIONS (1981) *Popular Participation as a Strategy for Promoting Community Level Action and National Development*, New York.

VITAL, D. (1975) *The Origins of Zionism*, Clarendon Press, Oxford.

WORLD BANK (1975) *The Assault on World Poverty*, John Hopkins University Press, Baltimore.

Documents and Newspapers (in Hebrew)

ALBEK, P. (1975) *A Final Report of Professional Team on the Issue of Land Arrangements in the Northern Negev*, Ministry of Justice, Jerusalem.

BEDOUIN TEAM (1979) *Meeting with the Bedouin*, 25.10.1979.

BEN GURION, D. (1948) 15.5.1948, *A Declaration of the Creation of the State of Israel*.
LERMAN, R. (1979) *Draft of Discussion for Settlement Arrangements with the Bedouin*, 14.3.1979.
LERMAN, R. (1979) *Meeting Agenda for the Bedouin*, 29.3.1979.
MINISTRY OF INTERIOR (1976) *Development Plan for the Negev*.
SHOSHANI, D. (1980) *Speech in Front of the Negev Committee*, 3.1.1980.
THE ASSOCIATION OF CIVIL RIGHTS IN ISRAEL (1979) *A Proposal for Land Arrangements*,
    4.4.1979.

Interviews

ABU AJAJ, M., Assistant of the Advisor of Arab Affairs in the Negev, Member of the Regional
    Council, resident of Kessifa (Beer Sheva, 15.6.1988 and Kessifa, 12.7.1988).
ABU HMED, S., Member of the regional council (Be'er Sheva, 19.7.1988).
ABU HMED, S., Sheikh of the Abu Hmed tribe (Be'er Sheva, 27.7.1988).
ABU MEEMER, A., Member of the regional council, resident of Segev Shalom (Be'er Sheva,
    20.8.1988).
ABU MTIR, I., Resident of Kessifa (Kessifa, 19.7.1988).
ABU REBEHA, A., Supervisor on the Bedouin education in the Ministry of Education (Beer
    Sheva, 17.8.1988).
ABU REBEHA, Y., Bedouin, Medical Doctor (Beer Sheva, 24.8.1988).
ABU SIAM, S., Bedouin agricultural planner in the Ministry of Agriculture, resident of Rahat
    (Beer Sheva, 18.8.1988).
ABU ZAALUK, Y., Member of the regional council, resident of Aruar (Be'er Sheva, 9.8.1988).
ALBEK, P., Manager of the Civil Department in the Ministry of Justice (Jerusalem, 29.8.1988).
AMIT, S. and KAPLAN, A., Planners of Rahat and Kessifa (Tel-Aviv, 22.7.1988).
ATZMON, E., Member of the Negotiation Team (Be'er Sheva, 20.6.1988).
BAR, A., The Deputy of the Director of Ministry of Housing, Be'er Sheva District (Be'er Sheva,
    4.7.1988).
BEN DAVID, J., Researcher, work with the Bedouin (Jerusalem, 13.6.1988).
BEN MEIR, M., Former Water Commissioner and the General Director of the Ministry of
    Agriculture — The head of the Implementation Authority (Tel-Aviv, 14.7.1988).
EL AMOUR, I., Sheikh of El Amour tribe, resident of Kessifa (Be'er Sheva, 27.7.1988).
GILBOHA, A., Advisor of Arab Affairs 1987–1989 (Jerusalem, 7.7.1988).
LERMAN, R., Planner of Aruar, member of the Negev Team and the Bedouin Team (Tel-Aviv,
    8.7.1988).
LIVNE, N., Social worker, lives in spontaneous settlement of Lekia (Lekia, 5.8.1988).
MARX, E., Anthropologist at the Tel Aviv University, member of the Bedouin Team (Tel Aviv,
    15.9.1988).
SAGEI, I., Former member of Negotiation Team, at present chairman of Masos Regional Council
    (Be'er Sheva, 29.6.1988).
SHOSHANI, D., Member of Kibbutz, Chief Negotiator in the Implementation Authority (Kibbutz
    Lahav, 15.6.1988).

LOCATION SCIENCE

Editors: **RICHARD CHURCH**, *Department of Geography, University of California at Santa Barbara, Santa Barbara, CA 93106, USA,* **JOHN CURRENT**, *Faculty of Management Sciences, College of Business, Ohio State University, 301 Hagerty Hall, 1775 College Road, Columbus, OH 43210-1399, USA* & **H. A. EISELT**, *Faculty of Administration, University of New Brunswick, PO Box 4400, Fredericton, NB, Canada E3B 5A3*

The primary focus of this journal is on research directed to extending and applying the theory and modeling of location decisions. The journal will also publish papers which address the underlying processes related to locational decisions, the determination of parameters associated with location problems, and issues of implementation. The submission of papers which apply locational constructs to non-locational problems is encouraged. In addition, the journal will occasionally publish articles reporting on specific applications of location modeling, as well as invited literature reviews and perspectives. These latter articles will include, but not be limited to, recommendations for future research, analysis of failures in past research and historical overviews.

Due to the complexity, strategic importance, and widespread application of location analysis, it has attracted the interest of researchers from many academic disciplines. These include economics, engineering, geography, logistics, marketing, mathematics, management information systems, operations research, regional science and planning, among others. It is intended that the journal will be representative of the various academic disciplines involved in location analysis. An important goal of the journal is to encourage interdisciplinary communication and research. Consequently, authors should write their papers in a style which is accessible to interested readers from disciplines other thana their own. This is not to imply that rigor should be sacrificed, but rather, that authors should take the time (and words) to explain their findings in a manner which is understandable to researchers in allied disciplines.

A Selection of Papers
G. O. WESOLOWSKY (Canada), The Weber problem: history and perspectives..
R. K. KINCAID (USA), The p-dispersion sum problem: results on trees and graphs.
R. D. GALVAO (Brazil), The use of Lagrangean relaxation in the solution of uncapacitated facility location problems.
D. SCHILLING (USA), A review of covering problems in facility location.
D. SERRA (Spain) & **C REVELLE** (USA), The P-Q median problem: location and districting of hierarchical facilities.

(00108)
Subscription Information
1993: Volume 1 (4 issues)
Annual subscription (1993)   £120.00   US$192.00*
ISSN: 0966-8349

PERGAMON PRESS
Pergamon Press Ltd, Headington Hill Hall, Oxford OX3 0BW, UK
Pergamon Press Inc., 660 White Plains Road, Tarrytown, NY 10591-5153, USA

A member of the Elsevier Science Publishing Group

First price quoted is definitive. Prices include postage and insurance. * Asterisked price is quoted for convenience only and is subject to exchange rate fluctuation.